Sri Lanka's Global Factory Workers

I0094052

In Sri Lanka, the Free Trade Zone (FTZ) employs thousands of unmarried rural women, and their migration has aroused deep anxieties over female morality and ideal conduct. This book focuses on the global factory workers based in the FTZ, and analyzes intersections of gender, class and sexuality by looking at the sexual lives and struggles of the female workers.

Exploring the alternative sexual world created by Sri Lanka's female global factory workers who engage in practices—such as premarital sex, unmarried cohabitation, and, to a lesser extent, lesbianism—that mainstream Sinhalese Buddhist culture considers taboo, the author demonstrates that the articulations of good and bad women in relation to sexual behavior has rendered global workers' sexual lives "unutterable," leading to zones of silence, contradictory articulations and performances. Taking the reader into the forbidden zones of sexual discourses, choices, acts, and texts enacted and expressed in visible arenas yet remain unseen, unread or misread by onlookers, the book critically investigate how cultural, economic and political processes are implicated in the construction and expression of working class female sexualities.

An important contribution to the field of gender studies, the book addresses issues surrounding sexuality, particularly how it is shaped by global production networks as well as patriarchal nationalist projects. It is of interest to students and scholars of South Asian Studies and Gender Studies.

Sandya Hewamanne teaches Anthropology at the Department of Sociology, University of Essex, UK. Her research interests include globalization, identity, cultural politics and feminist and post-colonial theory.

Routledge Contemporary South Asia Series

For a full list of titles in this series, please visit www.routledge.com

Sri Lanka's Global Factory Workers

(Un)Disciplined desires and sexual struggles in a post-colonial society

Sandya Hewamanne

Routledge
Taylor & Francis Group
LONDON AND NEW YORK

First published 2016
by Routledge
2 Park Square, Milton Park, Abingdon, Oxon OX14 4RN

and by Routledge
711 Third Avenue, New York, NY 10017

Routledge is an imprint of the Taylor & Francis Group, an informa business

Copyright © 2016 Sandya Hewamanne

British Library Cataloguing in Publication Data
A catalogue record for this book is available from the British Library

Library of Congress Cataloging-in-Publication Data
Names: Hewamanne, Sandya, author.
Title: Sri Lanka's global factory workers : (un) disciplined desires and
    sexual struggles in a post-colonial society / Sandya Hewamanne.
Description: New York : Routledge, 2016. | Series: Routledge
    contemporary South Asia series | Includes bibliographical references
    and index.
Identifiers: LCCN 2016002029 | ISBN 9780415819862 (hardback) |
    ISBN 9781315543741 (ebook)
Subjects: LCSH: Women—Sexual behavior—Sri Lanka. | Women—
    Employment—Sri Lanka.
Classification: LCC HQ29 .H49 2016 | DDC 306.7082095493—dc23
LC record available at https://lccn.loc.gov/2016002029

ISBN: 978-0-415-81986-2 (hbk)
ISBN: 978-0-367-86768-3 (pbk)

Typeset in Times New Roman
by Apex CoVantage, LLC

For two women, who in their own varied ways, shaped the woman I have become:

My mother Soma Hewamanne and my aunt Nirmala Herath

Contents

Acknowledgements

The sole reason I have been able to write this book is because the Katunayake Free Trade Zone (FTZ) workers I befriended over many years allowed me entry into their public and private spaces. Their strength, skill, and creativity when negotiating unpalatable situations even while contesting dominant cultural norms have long inspired me, and made this project an uplifting exercise. I will forever be grateful for their kindness, acceptance, affection, and sympathy.

I dearly hope local and global policymakers take note of these workers' predicaments and initiate policies to make exercising sexual and reproductive rights "normal." As for myself, I plan to use the material in this book to push relevant policymakers to pursue programs that empower global garment workers in Sri Lanka and elsewhere, and thereby partly pay back for my long research collaboration with the island's FTZ workers.

James and Judy Brow, Kamala Visweswaran, Polly Strong, and Kamran Ali have provided intellectual inspiration, mentorship, and friendship in equal measure through the years. Without them my career trajectory would have been quite different. My friends Ritu Khanduri, Denni Blum, Jenny Huberman, Bambi Chapin, Catherine Harnoise, Robin Simon, Ana Wahl, and Steve Gunkel have also influenced my work in various positive ways. I thank them all. A special thank you to Jenny Huberman for suggesting the book's provocative subheading.

My heartfelt gratitude to Anne Blackburn at Cornell University's South Asia Program for arranging a visiting scholar position in 2014 that provided a much needed change in intellectual climate that spurred me to finish this book. Portions of chapters 3, 4, and 5 were previously published in *Ethnography*, *Feminist Studies*, *Cultural Dynamics* and the book *Stitching Identities*. I thank the publishers for granting permission to reuse this material.

And then there is Neil and Sadie: thank you for lighting up my life!

1 Global factory workers and forbidden zones

The *Scent of the Lotus Pond* (*Bora Diya Pokuna*), a feature film by Satyajit Mai-tipe, portrays the intimate lives of three Free Trade Zone (FTZ) workers. One woman, Gothami, is not conventionally beautiful and is never the first choice for a man seeking a girlfriend. She lusts after her beautiful friend's boyfriend, Vipula, and has sex with him when he is drunk, sick, and sad. She gets pregnant, but Vipula thereafter reviles her and she is forced to abandon her baby at a train station. All three friends, together with others, flirt with and lead men on. Although the beautiful girl, Mangala, is able to marry her boyfriend, Vipula, she later reveals that she had an abortion when her affair with another man, while dating Vipula, resulted in pregnancy.

Bora Diya Pokuna contains sexually explicit scenes and dialogue when portraying Gothami's sexual agency and her subsequent humiliation at the hands of Vipula and his friends. This 2003 movie was banned in Sri Lanka until 2015. The reason, according to the director, was because it included "the first female masturbation scene ever." The censors, and by extension the government, were apparently afraid of publicly acknowledging that unmarried, young women have sexual desires and can freely express such desires. Many older people I talked to seemed to share this view, for they said the movie focused on the few "bad" girls in the FTZ to make money. While the movie, by depicting the three people who transgressed sexual norms being punished for their acts, ended up reiterating a common Buddhist understanding of the karmic cycle, also portrays rural to urban migrant women's lives in a manner that aroused intense anxieties among middle class people, older generations, and the government.

This book deals with such anxieties by exploring the alternative sexual world created by Sri Lanka's female global factory workers who engage in practices – such as premarital sex, unmarried cohabitation, and, to a lesser extent, lesbianism – that mainstream Sinhalese Buddhist culture considers taboo. This new articulation of desires, pleasure, and empowerment arouse deep fears over female morality and ideal conduct especially among Sri Lanka's elite but also among ordinary people, which they express through surveillance and by policing workers' behavior.

By showing how migrant factory workers manage sexual lives under the ever-present gaze of neighbors, police, NGOs, and middle class people and ascertain their citizenship rights within a subversive and unacknowledged public contesta-tory space, the book argues that articulations of good and bad women in relation to sexual behavior has rendered global workers' sexual lives "unutterable," lead-ing to zones of silence, contradictory articulations, and performances. I further argue that attempts to both express and constrain different forms of desire are linked to the macro-and-micro projects of global capitalism, nation-making, mili-tarization, and constructions of the self.

The book also considers how the spatial shifts from village to city and back to the village correspond to shifting images of FTZ women – ranging from obedient and virginal village daughters to promiscuous and fun-loving global workers to acceptable village daughters-in-law. The move from village to city allows women to jettison some aspects of internalized discipline and negotiate new desires. At the same time, the responses of certain agents and institutions that seek to dis-cipline the FTZ workers – elites, NGOs, middle class people – contribute to the ongoing stigma of FTZ work. These detractors simultaneously castigate the work-ers for their undisciplined behavior, use them as a foil against which to assert their own moral and disciplined desires, and attempt to reform or *save* these women (by controlling their desires). For the workers themselves, however, it is precisely by pursuing and enacting these seemingly "undisciplined" desires that they expe-rience new forms of pleasure, empowerment, and selves. By examining such tensions at length, the following chapters investigate how these female factory workers are implicated in global capitalism, nationalism, and militarization even as they push back against conditions that put them at a serious socio-economic disadvantage.

This book ultimately focuses on the sexualities of the marginalized by going beyond the official and popular discourses to discuss intimate spaces of global workers' lives. It illustrates how these women's sexual desires battle against their internalized Sinhala Buddhist nationalist notions of what it means to be good girls and the impact this has on psychic, social, and physical realms of their daily lives. I seek to take the reader into the forbidden zones of sexual discourses, choices, acts, and texts enacted and expressed in visible arenas yet remain unseen, unread, or misread by onlookers. By focusing on this misreading, I seek to critically investigate how cultural, economic, and political processes are implicated in the construction and expression of working class female sexualities.

The Free Trade Zone

Sri Lanka's first FTZ was established in Katunayake in 1978, and thousands of unmarried rural women have worked there and at several others established later in Biyagama and Koggala.[1] Outsourcing assembly line work to factories in third world countries was based on several patriarchal assumptions about gendered lives: women in these countries are docile and nimble fingered and would not rebel against low salaries and boring repetitive work; they are supplementary earners and therefore do not need a full pay package; and they have husbands, fathers, and brothers who take care of their basic housing, food, and health needs.

The government at the time went one step further and added certain rules and regulations through the Board of Investment (BOI), the body that was created to oversee investments in Sri Lankan FTZs. One rule was based on the belief that FTZ assembly line work would allow young women to earn enough for their dowry. This led to workers being able to collect their accumulated Employee Provident Fund (EPF) and Employee Trust Fund (ETF) together with company gratuity payments, provided they had worked for more than five years and could produce marriage certificates within three months of leaving employment. This branded the FTZ as a source of employment best suited for unmarried women from poor families even as it pushed women eager to collect the lump sum payments into hasty marriages. It also helped factories get rid of assertive and politically conscious FTZ workers after five or six years of work and hire new workers from rural areas.

While such patriarchal contours sought to dictate cultural, physical, and psychic parameters and shape workers' lives while at the FTZ, the women fought back in creative ways. This book explores their agency while analyzing how seemingly private matters such as sexual relations and reproductive decision-making are connected to national, patriarchal, and global capitalist hegemonies. More importantly, it shows how these rural, young women who willingly became the lowest rung of global assembly lines contest dominant culture through nuanced, interwoven mechanisms. It also focuses on how women conform, resist and play with the positions that they are called to occupy by fashioning identities. Neoliberalism is supposed to make existing hierarchies obsolete. These women workers' struggles to create meaningful sexual lives, however, show that neoliberalism is still embroiled in a battle with existing ideologies, beliefs, and norms.

The stigma and low salaries associated with FTZ work were a major reason that urban young women stayed away from FTZ factory jobs, thus increasing opportunities for rural women who migrated far from home to take up these jobs. The jobs not only provided these rural women an income they were unable to earn in their villages, but FTZ work was considered better than going abroad (typically to the Middle East) to work as domestic help. As the first batch of migrant workers brought back money, knowledges, new styles and tastes back home, others followed them to Katunayake.

The women who thus migrated from their rural villages to the urban areas took up residence in hastily built rows of boarding rooms local residents provided. The dominant image of the ideal woman – which was mostly constructed during the anti-colonial movement in the late nineteenth and early twentieth centuries – is a subordinate who must be protected within the confines of her home. But this understanding stigmatized women who migrated to the urban FTZs to live and work on their own without family supervision.

Sri Lankan children are socialized into practices of shame-fear – to be ashamed to subvert norms of sexual modesty and proper behavior, and to fear the social ridicule that results from such subversion. In particular, young women's behavior is measured by their adherence to such norms and practices. But by living away from their parents and staying together with other working women in female-only boarding houses around the FTZ, women acquired new knowledges that were previously considered taboo, causing their cognitive, social, emotional, and moral dispositions to change.

In addition to developing political consciousness within the factories, these women quickly learned to subvert cultural norms and explore sexual desires and pleasures. While new forms of sexualities flourished openly within the FTZ area (the actual barbed-wire fenced FTZ, and the surrounding area, which consisted of boarding houses and commercial and public spaces that catered to the workers – the bazaar, main bus terminal, city streets, and the railroad), the mainstream media and other interested parties sought to suppress public expression of erotic and sexual acts. They also took steps to deny female workers' desires, voices, and agency in shaping this sexual subculture, by claiming they were all victims of unscrupulous men.

National elites have bought into a narrative influenced by the anti-colonial movement that claims village women are bearers of authentic, pure Sinhala Buddhist culture and hence embody the nation-state. They, consequently, pin any blame pertaining to sexual indiscretions on a few, claiming that wayward women who let predatory urban men take advantage of them end up giving the mainly good and moral female work force a bad name. The workers, however, capitalize on this contradiction by enjoying new sexualities even as they side with the discursively constructed group of "innocent, good garment workers" whenever it benefits them. Their ability to manage transgressions and good reputations simultaneously also benefit global capitalism and the interests of the national elite by ensuring that a steady flow of rural women remain available to work in low-wage, low-security, transnational assembly lines.

The frequent transgressions of conventional moral values do not mean that the women workers have it easy; for many are the institutions and agents that participate in an elaborate informal surveillance network focused on their lives. While women have always had to deal with the paternalistic gaze, FTZ area policing has more to do with suppressing bold expressions of sexuality than eliminating them altogether. Many agents associated with national and local governing bodies and culture – police, military officials, NGO and civil society personnel, bureaucrats, and teachers – are poised between the working and middle classes, and they take the opportunity to condemn women's sexual activities and thereby make themselves look superior. They relish the opportunity to render their services in "saving wayward daughters." The book explores the highly creative ways in which workers respond to these efforts to "save" ' them while managing both their transgressions and reputations. Most of their transgressions are intertwined with their performances of conformity, thus enacting an intricate drama of (non) discipline.

The book also highlights how workers perceive, understand, and appreciate talented women who take advantage of available social and sexual opportunities without getting into trouble (i.e., becoming pregnant), faithfully take care of their responsibilities toward natal families in the village, and safeguard their reputations by marrying boyfriends or someone chosen by parents. This alternative ideal and long-term empowerment are significantly circumscribed by the temporary character of their jobs, which requires them to return to their villages after a few years, and by mainstream expectations that a good woman is a virgin at marriage. I discuss how these constraints shape the way women strategize their romantic and intimate lives and the emotional and physical violence they suffer as a result.

Researching workers, researching culture

The book is based on long-term ethnographic research conducted from 2000–2015. In 2000, I resided in a boarding house for FTZ garment workers for 11 months and worked at a FTZ garment factory for seven months. During this time, I volunteered at two Katunayake NGO offices and also followed workers back to their villages when they went on long vacations. I continued to visit the FTZ area during the summer and winter breaks of nearly all subsequent years. During these field visits I focused, among other issues, on the FTZ's sexual sub-culture and how elites and other powerful sections of society responded to it. While staying with these women in boarding houses, I was able to closely observe how romantic and intimate relationships start, develop, and, more often than not, collapse. I witnessed the emotional outbursts that ensue when romances break up, abandonments occur, unwanted pregnancies leading to abortions at illegal road-side clinics take place, and how these tragedies sometimes result in suicide threats and attempts enacted publicly.

I went shopping and to musical shows with these women workers and accom-panied them on long road trips and witnessed how their relationships blossomed, peaked, and crashed. I attended to them after they returned from abortions or threatened to commit suicide (attempts that were usually enacted dramatically), and provided a sympathetic ear when they talked about the pleasures and pains associated with intimate relationships. In the crowded, congested environment of the boarding houses, it was hard not to be part of their pornographic magazine reading sessions and joking, singing, and poetry-reciting circles. I went with them to the police station to complain about boyfriends who stole from them, or to speak on behalf of women workers who were accused of "inappropriate behav-ior" in public. I was fortunate that many workers shared stories of their sexual lives and even their journals with me. It is their countless ruminations about the complexities of managing desires and reputations that partly inform this book. In addition, I have conducted in-depth interviews and focus groups with women workers. I usually conducted interviews and focus groups with women who were available and willing at varied boarding houses at a given time. In 2012, 2013, and 2014 I used narratives of three NGO activists, who worked closely with some women workers experiencing difficulties relating to premarital sex, shared with me to select 12 workers for life history interviews.

Many of these women often become isolated in villages still steeped in patri-archal ideals once they leave the FTZ and, with time, the economic, social, and cultural empowerment garnered within the FTZ appear to wither away. Since 2003 I have also been investigating how these former workers reintegrate into their villages as prospective brides, new wives, and young mothers. I have participated in former workers' gendered social activities and expressive practices (story-telling, joking, singing) to see how they express or constrain desires within everyday life once back in their villages. I collected their narratives and interviewed their relatives, in-laws, and neighbors to discern how former workers and others delicately dance around the issue of the "undisciplined" FTZ worker who has now become their "overly conforming" in-law or neighbor. It is all these years of interviews and field work within and outside the FTZ that informs the chapters that follow.

Changing free trade zones

According to the General Services Employees Union Joint Secretary, Mr. Anton Marcus, the International Trade Union Confederation's Annual Report to the World Trade Organization notes that "Sri Lanka had ratified all 8 core ILO labor conventions, but has fallen short of implementing these conventions and continues to restrict trade union rights".[2] Prohibiting political organizations within global factories is one of the main problems associated with global assembly lines. This not only allows for labor and human rights violations within factories to go unchallenged, it also reproduces the strict patriarchal structures within which global production operates.

As noted above, the first FTZ in Sri Lanka was established in 1978. It fulfilled a 1977 election promise the United National Party (UNP) made when it campaigned on a platform of opening markets and welcoming foreign investors to the country. To attract investors to the FTZ, the newly established BOI touted the availability of "well-disciplined and obedient women workers, who can produce more in a short time" (Dabindu Collective 1997). Similarly, the FTZ jobs were promoted among Sri Lankan rural young women as a way to earn a wage, learn new things, and save for dowries. As a result, thousands of rural young women migrated to the area seeking work. The notion that women facing no other choice would accept employment under any condition and that they are secondary or supplementary wage earners resulted in minimal wages and rigorous work schedules. As in other FTZs around the world (Fernandez-Kelly 1983; Pena 1997; Mills 1999; Salzinger 2003; Pun 2005), transnational companies in the Katunayake FTZ demand maximum output for minimal wages in extremely exploitative working conditions. In 2003, the Katunayake FTZ contained 92 transnational factories. At that time about 50,000 were employed within FTZ factories, while around 70,000 more were employed by subcontracting factories located around the Katunayake area. In 2014, according to officials at the BOI, about 30,000 young women were employed in factories within the zone, while around 40,000 were employed by subcontracting factories located in its vicinity.[3] The termination of the Multi-Fiber Agreement (MFA), which put a halt to preferential exports to the United States in 2013, and suspension of the Generalized Scheme of Preferences Plus status (which allowed garment exports with little or no tariffs) with the European Union, due to the government's poor human rights record had resulted in many factories exiting Sri Lanka.

Well-known companies such as Mas Holdings setting up factories in other parts of the country also facilitated this drastic drop in the numbers employed around Katunayake. However, the number of women who do part time work (called "manpower workers") has significantly increased over the last two years, so the official numbers are actually lower than the actual number of workers around the FTZ. Today some workers prefer to engage in part time work, an option factories promote because it absolves them from providing health and safety benefits. But this adversely affects permanent workers' struggles for more labor rights.

In referring to the factory of the future, Anil Hidramani, Director of Hidramani Group of Garment Factories, notes that "the consumer is demanding clothing, faster, better and cheaper" and, therefore, fast fashion, where a retailer is able to "develop a new product in one week," is what the future will be. This will in turn lead to fewer workers and technology (robotics) playing a major role in apparel production (July 2015).[4] This future most certainly seems bleak for workers and countries dependent on assembly line production.

But there is better news for now. In July 2015 the US Congress re-authorized the generalized system of preferences for Sri Lanka along with 122 other countries. The defeat of President Mahinda Rajapaksa in January 2015 and the subsequent parliamentary victory by a UNP-led coalition has especially been welcomed by Western countries, and many in the garment sector now hope that the European Union GSP Plus benefits will also be reintroduced. Irrespective of these developments, the social, economic, and cultural contexts surrounding global workers' lives that I note below are not likely to change soon.

As noted above, at the beginning there were few state or factory-run hostel facilities for women who flocked to the FTZ, leading to people living in the area renting out hastily-built rows of rooms to women. Although 37 years later some factories now provide limited hostel facilities for new workers, the majority of FTZ workers continue to live in insecure, poorly built, and overcrowded rooms with poor access to running water, electricity, and health and sanitary services. Such shortcomings make life in the FTZ difficult. The physically and mentally arduous target-oriented production structure also contributes to labor and human rights violations within factories, which go unchallenged, because trade union activity is curtailed or absent (Dabindu Collective 1997; Gunawardana 2010; Ruwanpura 2011; Hewamanne 2012).

Instead of the violation of workers' rights and their poor living conditions, the public attention has obsessed over their status as young women living alone devoid of male protection. Popular accounts of widespread premarital sex, rape, prostitution, abortion, infanticide, and attempted suicide simultaneously portray these women both as victims of sexual exploitation and as victims of their own loose morals. Workers are identified in everyday discourses as "garment girls" and are said to be recognizable by their dress, hair styles, and language. So many young women congregating in one place is such an unusual phenomenon that people call the FTZ *Sthri Puraya* (city of women), *Prema Kalape* (love zone), and *Vesa Kalape* (whore zone). Their neighbors in the FTZ area brand global workers living amidst them as "free living women," who (as a group) represent a "great disaster" (Hewamanne 2008a). Such intense anxieties about their morality has created an image of FTZ workers being women with loose virtues who can be easily deceived into having sexual relationships.

While politicians promoted FTZ work as an avenue for rural youth to attain modernity, women workers found it almost impossible to secure symbols (apart from some items of clothing) of modernity using their meager salaries. According to an undated BOI document on "Industrial Factor Costs" that became available in 2006, skilled Sri Lankan workers were paid between Rs. 2,500–3,250 while non-skilled workers were paid Rs. 2,000–2,500. The basic salary of a FTZ worker was Rs. 2,250 (about US$25) per month, but workers could earn about Rs. 3,000–4,000 by working overtime and not taking their annual leave. In 2015, the basic salary was around Rs. 7,000 (approximately $50.00) for differently skilled workers, and with overtime and incentives, a hard working woman could make about Rs. 20,000 (about $140.00) per month. Unfortunately, inflation has approximated salary increases, rendering the higher pay meaningless. For instance, a boarding room that was shared among four women cost Rs. 1,200 per month per person in 1999 (approximately $16.00 at the time); the same room cost about Rs. 3,600 (about $ 25.00) per person per month in 2015. The increase in food prices also approximated the salary increase.

Among the FTZ workers I interviewed over the years, only a few had parents and family that made heavy financial demands on them, unlike the parents of Javanese and Thai FTZ workers (Wolf 1992; Mills 1999). However, what Sri Lankan workers received as salary was only a little above survival wage and did not help much in achieving highly desirable ways of living. As noted above, most FTZ factory owners expected workers to leave the factory after five years of employment with the accumulated EPF, ETF, and five year bonus payments the factory gave them. Indeed, even when some women wanted to keep on working, social pressure made it difficult to do so because it caused people to suggest their preference was dictated by no men desiring their hand in marriage. Though couched in the rhetoric of marriage and motherhood, the institutional push toward leaving jobs after five years enabled factory owners to recruit fresh batches of younger workers and get rid of senior workers who were becoming politically conscious. This evidences how conventional gender norms are employed to further global capitalist interests.

Although the challenges associated with FTZ work may outweigh overall gains, a stagnant agricultural economy, lack of alternative employment, and the allure of modernity and urban living styles (which television does a great job of promoting) also appears to influence the move to the FTZ. Many workers nearing their five to six years of employment dread going back to their villages and wish there was a way to live fulfilling lives while continuing to work at the FTZ. This demonstrates that many among these workers, notwithstanding the drudgery of assembly line work, value the independence and wage worker identity the FTZ has facilitated. But this is precisely what unnerves those among the cultural police seeking to discipline women's desires and bodies.

Katunayake neighbors, police, and NGOs

The rapid urbanization and industrialization of Katunayake that resulted from FTZ transnational production and related globalized socio-cultural flows affected its residents' lived experiences in varied ways. State authorities did little planning to accommodate the new migrant population to this area and instead expected these village women to find their own accommodations among neighboring families, partly because they believed these women were sexually ignorant, had a strict sense of shame-fear, and thus needed the family environment. While busy exploiting the new economic opportunities that followed the influx of rural women, neighbors also reinvented themselves as moral guardians of the newcomers. Many other agents and institutions – including the media, police, NGOs, and researchers – involved themselves in the spatial and conceptual production of the new city and its gendered citizen subjects.

Katunayake is located about an hour away from Colombo's main bus terminal and belongs to the Gampaha District. Although home to the country's only international airport, it remained a minor town council (*sulu nagara sabha*) until 1977, when the government decided to establish the first FTZ there. The area now covered by the FTZ had been surrounded by villages without running water or electricity. The open economy and other structural adjustments led to Katunayake's inclusion in what was officially referred to as the Greater Colombo Economic Plan, with peculiar consequences for local politics: for while still an electorate of Gampaha District, it received differential infrastructure development. This led to Katunayake inheriting good roads, warehouses, numerous small factories, and a number of national and some international banks – all designed to cater to the clientele associated with the FTZ. A consumer culture also soon developed around the FTZ, spawning shops, eateries, folk religious healers, pavement hawkers, a Sunday bazaar, and music and other entertainment activities – all catering exclusively to FTZ workers (Hewamanne 2008b).

Spatial ordering has long been a strategy of registering social distance (Caldeira 1999; Low 2001; Smart 2001). In the case of the FTZ, the economic activities the FTZ workers helped generate allowed most local families to acquire and flaunt middle class accoutrements. Several families who earned enough moved out of the area while still renting their Katunayake houses to FTZ workers. Others started displaying such demarcations as barbed wire fences that separated the boarding house area from the owner's house while still letting the owners supervise tenants' behavior. Many city dwellers disdained and stayed away from the social arenas such as the shopping junction, bazaar, eateries, and other recreational spaces created for, and shaped by, FTZ workers.

The workers, however, enthusiastically consumed the public spaces built around their lives. On weekends, they went to Aweriwatte Junction to buy food and shop, to have their horoscopes read, or to socialize. Venders catered to the throngs of women and groups of young men following them. Women gathered in circles by the roadside, bus stops, and shop fronts to engage in loud conversations while young men gathered near them and exchanged jokes. The appropriation of public space for such activities has always been contested, and when the group is socially marginalized, it especially generates fear and anxiety among the middle classes. City streets have been a site of social struggle as far back as the early nineteenth century, with the middle classes opposing those who congregated to socialize or participate in parades (Peiss 1986; Domosh 1998; Enstad 1999). It was no different in Katunayake.

The particular social relations and cultural practices in a space define and label it. How workers choose to use specific spaces around the FTZ, encompassing the immediate vicinity of the actual FTZ factory compound, caused these locations to be reconceived as sites of gendered resistance where women challenge cultural norms. These spaces were also stigmatized as places where women behave boisterously, unlike good, innocent village women, and where women unabashedly express erotic desires. Neighbors, most of whom achieved social mobility on the back of FTZ related economic activities, devised numerous little ways of marking differences between them and the rural to urban migrant industrial workers so as to preserve their own precarious new class positioning. Most significant among them was a rigid, intensified sense of what it is to be a good woman, through which they measured workers' behavior, decided on the degree of surveillance, and meted out punishments.

As noted above, ideals pertaining to what constitutes a good, unmarried woman were constructed during the anti-colonial movement in the late nineteenth and early twentieth centuries in response to British representations of Sri Lankan women and culture. This ideal projected women as passive and subordinate beings who should be protected within the confines of their homes. As a result, women leaving their parental homes to live alone in urban, modernized spaces aroused intense anxieties about cultural degradation and female morality.

This combination of Victorian sensibilities, Indian patriarchal traditions, and local ideal type behaviors that prescribed "decent and correct" manners and morals, as well as a proper attitude toward sexuality for middle class women, was eagerly subscribed to by Sri Lanka's own nationalist leaders. These men – and they were all men – of the early twentieth century nationalist movement felt that instilling virtues of Victorian femininity, domesticity, discipline, and restraint was necessary if they were to transform Sinhala Buddhist women, and through them the island, into a symbol of national greatness. Among the nationalists Anagarika Dharmapala played a significant role in recasting women as religious, moral, educated, and accomplished. He introduced new dress codes, rules of comportment and ideas on general hygiene and good housekeeping for women (Guruge 1965; De Alwis 1997). When comingled with anti-imperialist rhetoric, many sections of society enthusiastically embraced these codes of gendered behavior.

Sinhala Buddhist young women are expected to be virgins at the time of marriage and are ideally expected to be ignorant of all forms of sexual knowledge until marriage. This importance given to virginity also contributed to the anxieties over women living alone in the city and having unsupervised leisure time because it provided the opportunity to transgress norms relating to premarital sex.

A discursively constructed notion regarding the moral superiority of the village as the locus of tradition put an additional burden on rural women (Moore
1985; Brow 1999). Such superimposed notions of superior morals and undis-
turbed traditions initiated expectations that village women are naïve, innocent (in
the sense of being sexually ignorant), timid and were the unadulterated bearers
of Sinhala Buddhist culture. When such women migrated to the city and started
enjoying their time away from patriarchal control, fears about their morality
became a major preoccupation for urban, middle class people. Like nationalists
in many other post-colonial societies, they considered any threat to women's
morality a threat against the nation's cultural purity (Chatterjee 1993; Yuval-
Davis 1997, 2012).

Although Sri Lanka has witnessed massive social, economic, and political
changes since the early twentieth century, ideals pertaining to good womanly
behavior have not changed much. Women belonging to different social classes
negotiate, resist, and readjust these ideals in their daily lives in varied ways, yet as
a general standard the expectations noted above remain well and alive. Obviously,
the socio-economic circumstances of working class women are not conducive to
following dominant norms of respectability, but in verbal and written expressions
all Sinhala women (and to an extent Tamil and Muslim women) are measured
by this unitary notion of respectability. FTZ garment factory workers, who are
predominantly rural women now living in the city unrestrained by village norms,
therefore come under harsh criticism, and their conduct has become the space
where deep anxieties and ambivalences over notions of development, modernity,
and sexuality are played out.

According to Obeyesekere (1984), Sinhala children are socialized into practices of shame-fear (*lajja-baya*) – to be ashamed of subverting norms of sexual
modesty and proper behavior and to fear the social ridicule that result from such
subversion – from a young age (504–505). When women started migrating to the
cities for FTZ work, it was the impact on their *lajja-baya* that the middle class and
males feared most. Many felt the FTZ workers' public behavior proved that they
had lost the internalized sense of shame-fear, thus becoming shameless women
(sluts). As the stigma deepened, thanks to exaggerated stories of women living
carefree love lives by indulging in rampant premarital sex and unmarried cohabitation, more and more men entered the area with the expressed purpose of finding FTZ girlfriends. Stories of date rape, unwanted pregnancies, and infanticide
featured prominently in the national media, which condemned FTZ workers as
victims of unscrupulous men and as victims of their own frivolous desires. These
perceptions and the resulting individual, group, and geographical stigma shaped
women's experience, expressions, and desires, while simultaneously framing
efforts designed to repress them.

Just like many Katunayake neighbors, the police, NGO members, and jour-
nalists who came looking for stories belonged to either the middle class or to
upwardly mobile working class families that are steeped in mainstream notions
of female behavior. For example, an article in the Dabindu NGO's magazine
(June 2000) focused on a suicide death of a FTZ worker and wrote, she "came

to the city a charming rural woman" and "became a cancelled coin" in the hands of a married lover. Although dedicated to improving labor conditions, some of these staff members found it difficult to jettison their own internalized dominant cultural expectations, and many articles that addressed social problems in the FTZ area contained material demonstrating a patriarchal understanding of female morality.

The NGOs no doubt provide FTZ workers a certain space to develop and raise their voices, but in some other ways constrain their political voice from blossoming, specifically in the realm of erotic desires. The dynamics of such constraints varied according to the NGO structure and the individual staff member. For example, an NGO magazine in the area, *Niveka*, sometimes carried articles containing alternative views on young people's sexual desires and non-nationalistic views on the island's civil war. Overall, however, almost all NGOs followed dominant cultural norms when it came to understanding sex and held that women workers should refrain from sexual activities for their own good. Belonging to middle or upwardly mobile working classes, many staff members struggled to see beyond internalized cultural norms. Even the few who saw sexual freedom as a human right thought this particular group of women (as opposed to urban, upper middle class women) should refrain from publicly expressing transgressions for their own safety and for ensuring an unsullied reputation.

Beginning with the civil war in 1983 Sri Lanka experienced periods of intense hostilities, ceasefires, and peace talks, until a comprehensive government military effort saw the war end controversially in May 2009. During this time the government fanned nationalistic fervor by promoting the image of the selfless, patriotic war-hero. The intensified ethno-nationalistic feelings added another layer of complexity to the demands on rural women living in urban areas. As bearers of authentic Sinhala Buddhist traditions, the women workers were supposed to display their patriotism by adhering to traditions upholding female conduct. The police stationed around the FTZs, therefore, took it upon themselves to not only keep law and order in the area but to police the women's behavior. This saw the Katunayake, Seeduwa, and Negambo police stations adding special female personnel starting in the 1980s to deal with specific problems associated with the FTZ worker population. However, the women police personnel's interactions were also shaped by dominant cultural norms, social class positioning, aspirations of social mobility, and the stigma associated with FTZ work. Although many police personnel were from similar social class backgrounds as the FTZ workers, almost all of them, especially female cops, strictly aligned themselves with the middle class and operated as a force geared toward disciplining and educating the workers about middle class norms.

Owing to the close proximity of the Katunayake International Airport, the FTZ area registers a significant visibility of military personnel. While they mostly sought to take advantage of the easily available female worker population for their own needs, their very presence during the war shaped women's expressions of desire in interesting ways. These circumstances added layers of complexity to the workers' quest to achieve desired sexual lives.

Desire in its context

> In order to perpetuate itself, every oppression must corrupt or distort those vari-
> ous sources of power within the culture of the oppressed that can provide energy
> for change. For women, this has meant the suppression of the erotic as a considered
> source of power and information within our lives.
>
> (Lorde 2007: 53)

Audrey Lorde's statement applies perfectly to the particular context in Sri
Lanka that I am writing about. Sri Lankan women of all ethnic groups and
social classes are expected to be ignorant of sexual matters before marriage, be
restrained and reticent about expressing desires when married, and be in charge
of controlling young women's sexual expressions when older. Women of different groups negotiate these expectations, usually within flexible boundaries, in
their own ways in everyday life. Still open exploration, expressions, and actions
are repressed and bound to bring severe social punishments on individuals and
their families. Rural women who migrate from non-anonymous, surveillance-
oriented villages to the FTZ area, where they can become one among many
migrant women, gradually become capable of jettisoning certain internalized mechanisms of repression and expressing erotic desires in varied ways.
Although still expressed within patriarchal contours, they display more open-
ness and agency than non-migrant women in recognizing and seeking fulfilment
of intertwined physical, emotional, and social desires. Most of them ultimately
desire the socially sanctioned end result of marriage with their partners. Yet,
agents of dominant cultural institutions still find their actions threatening and so
seek to repress their desires and actions.

Before we proceed further, it is important to figure out how I use desire in this
book. According to Deleuze and Guattari (1983), desire is decentered, pragmatic,
and dynamic in nature. Operating within a "domain of free synthesis" (54), it
seeks more objects, connections, and relations than any society can allow, leading
the latter to repress desire within closed cultural codes. Liberation of desire by
overcoming repressive cultural codes is thus important when seeking to reverse
traditional structures of subordination (139).

When I use desire in this book, I do not take erotic desire as a state of mind
that is divorced from emotional, psychic, and social contexts. The reason is that
the way FTZ workers felt, understood, and expressed their mostly heterosexual
desires was very tightly intertwined with their need for emotional satisfaction,
identity, social protection, and security. Almost all workers expressed their desire
to find a significant other with whom to have a deep connection that is physical
and emotional. They also hoped against hope that their relationships would end up
in the ultimate socially desired form of union: legal marriage. Many workers' relationships were formed not on sexual desire but the social desirability of a potential
partner, such as stable jobs, good upbringing, decent manners, etc. A substantial
number of workers knew that they wanted boyfriends as part of their social identity, and as a support system in a patriarchal society where a single woman in public spaces faced many dangers. At the same time, they desired physical intimacy

(kissing, touching, hugging) without necessarily recognizing a need or yearning for sexual intercourse. In many instances women in relationships felt that they had connected with their boyfriends at a deeper level and felt one with each other by together resisting the desire for sexual intercourse. Many women felt that by helping men masturbate (via oral sex or fondling) they actually engaged in intercourse and that the bonding thereby created made it incumbent on the men to marry them. They almost always held that it is the men they were with who desired sex and they had no choice but comply.

These perceptions of desire are definitely different from the erotic and sexual desires described by theorists who focus on Western societies. This makes it important to discuss the politics of passion, sex, and gender of the particular location. It has been noted that belief systems and the institutions that represent such beliefs pattern expressions of sexuality and shape desire and pleasure (Manderson and Aggleton 2003). The overwhelming majority of FTZ workers are either Buddhist by religion or have been brought up in a society steeped within a Buddhist ethos. One commonly used couplet of Buddha's sayings among Sri Lankans is *thanhaya jayathi soko* (desire brings sadness); *thanhaya jayathi bayan* (desire brings fear). According to Buddhist mythology, Thanha (desire), Rathi (lust), Ranga (entertainment) are the three daughters of Death (*mara*) who came to tempt Buddha and prevent him from attaining enlightenment. The stories relating to Buddha's former lives (*jathaka katha*) are also full of tales where men and women put themselves in humiliating or dangerous situations due to physical desires. Buddhists in Sri Lanka internalize the morals dictated by these stories at an early age and their upbringing is conditioned by such morals. Bambi Chapin (2014), while writing about the way boisterous, demanding young Sinhala Buddhist children who showed universal symptoms of "terrible twos" became restrained, calm, undemanding school children, describes how their socialization focuses on thwarting individual desires by using Buddhist parables and ethos.

Folk tales especially add to the fear and anxieties of desire created by the Buddhist *jathaka* stories. For instance, one popular saying among Sinhala people is "love *illow wenewa*" (love leads to funerals). A popular couplet that many young Sinhala girls wrote in their school-leaving autograph books was, "however beautiful the flower niyagla; you would die if you eat the niyagala tuber." Although not directly expressed, young women seem to be warning each other that something as beautiful as romantic love contains the danger of sex (eating the tuber), which will (socially) kill the person. Considering the high suicide and attempted suicide rates in Sri Lankan rural areas and the number of people using niyagala tuber to kill themselves, the couplet seems to allude to literal death as well.[5]

Religious and folk beliefs still influence state policies pertaining to rape, abortion, pornography, public indecency, and sex work because the government, the police, and the judiciary are heavily influenced by social norms based on these moral values. Education institutions and media further reiterate these notions when it comes to sexuality, desires, and pleasures. With this understanding of dangers associated with desire, it is perhaps not surprising that female FTZ workers'

expressions of desire were riddled with contradictions and ambivalences that differed from Western expressions.

However, it would be a mistake to assume that formal religious and folk
beliefs are completely repressive. Seemingly rigid institutions allow certain
transgressions to exist as long as they are expressed within manageable boundaries. Individuals and groups figure out what is allowed, not through socialization alone but also based on trial and error. When village women migrate
to FTZs and experience different social realities, they begin to question such
familiar codes, leading to newer ways of configuring acceptable expressions.
This is because desire, be it for sex, self-knowledge, social mobility, or power,
is culturally and historically conditioned and connected to reproducing, challenging, and recreating normative gender roles and identities (Greenberg 1995;
Murray 1999; Hewamanne 2012).

This book therefore explores how garment workers confronted the tensions created by competing ideologies, massive political economic transformations, and
resultant social realities to re-conceptualize local notions of desire and create possibilities for new meanings and social codes concerning sexualities. The *Special
Issue on Belief Systems and the Place of Desire: Perspectives from Asia and the
Pacific* (2003), among other studies, have explored how people in different social
contexts give meaning to desire within competing ideologies. Scholars have also
studied how new ideologies germinate new understandings of intimacy, desire,
and sex in South Asia (Vanita 2002; Ahearn 2003; Srivastava 2004; Bose 2008;
Arondekar 2009; Shah 2014). For instance, Western ideas and institutions shaped
understandings of sexuality and desire in colonial and post-colonial South Asia.
Chatterjee (1993) demonstrated how, as a response to colonial discourses, the
Bengali nationalists discursively reconstituted women and home as the location
of tradition by separating the material, public sphere dominated by the Europe-
ans and the spiritual domestic sphere where women upheld traditions. According
to Usha Zakharias, Gandhi's reworking of the myth of Ramayana[6] invoked the
figure of Sita as representing the feminine "uncolonizable" domain of the nation.
Gandhi saw Sita as a woman who resisted and renounced royal pleasures offered
by her captor Ravana, a metaphor used to refer to British culture and consumer
goods. This ensured middle and upper class Indian women's entry into the public sphere as spiritual, de-sexualized women who are "uncolonizable" and thus
resistant to that which threatened tradition (2001). In Sri Lanka too, women, and
rural women in particular, are considered the bearers of *authentic* Sinhala Buddhist culture and are expected not to be swayed negatively by new ideas, goods,
and practices. The Katunayake FTZ, being a place where rural, unmarried women
congregated and configured new ways of living and wage worker identities, thus
created anxieties about unwanted cultural changes. Such anxieties then went on to
shape the dynamics of women's intimate lives in interesting ways.

The last four decades has seen globalization and neoliberalism impose ideas
that disrupt traditional norms throughout South Asia, thereby creating tensions and
possibilities for adjusted meanings. Despite these social changes, women expressing desire is still considered an anomaly, and global workers find it difficult to talk

about their own physical desires. This, in turn, leads their expressions to remain at the performative level. Sexual activities thus get mostly described in culturally acceptable tropes, for example, saying this or that took place "due to pressure from men." As I explain later, the absence of everyday terms denoting sexual acts and desire that do not have negative connotations complicates the possibility of verbalizing desire.

Judith Butler argues that the reason some forms of sexuality lack a good vocabulary is because the powerful forces that determine how we think about desire, sexual acts, and pleasures do not admit to certain modes of sexuality (2009: iii). It is these same forces that determine some forms of sexual life as more possible than others, thereby making sure the disapproved forms are unthinkable or unutterable. This is also the case when it comes to FTZ workers and premarital sex.

As unmarried women in a society where premarital sex is taboo, many women found it impossible to experience the desire for sex or to enjoy sex. The social norm of denying premarital sexual desire is so powerful and deeply internalized that many were often unable to recognize desire until a later point in life, such as after marriage. Some new workers found the conflict of physical desires and normative codes so un-bearable that trances, fainting, and crying spells ensued in boarding houses. These women's articulations of desire are shaped by historical, cultural and nationalistic discourses; their own localized, marginalized understandings; and the neoliberal discourses they are saturated with. This leads to contradictions and ambivalences, making it difficult for onlookers or the participants in this scenario to find order, or to apply definite labels such as "coerced sex" or "consensual sex."[7]

Similarly, in writing about migrant Sri Lankan domestic workers in Lebanon, Monica Smith (2010) notes how state and non-state actors continually regulate and control the intimate and sexual lives of Sri Lankan migrant women in Beirut, leading to the erasure of non-normative sexual experiences. These very conditions make women's expressions of desire acutely political. As Lorde notes, restricting women's sexuality erases a significant source of their liberating power (2007). Therefore, the efforts to resurrect that liberating power are acutely political. FTZ women who are contesting acceptable limits by expressing desires are engaged in a subaltern political project that will shape what it means to be a good woman and a citizen with equal rights. It is their struggle and its influence on the changing economic, cultural, and political background that I chronicle in the chapters that follow.

Partying between a rock and a hard place

VARUNIKA: Of course, I loved the kissing and hugging part. But during that beach trip when he tried to touch me underneath my skirt, I jumped and ran away to where my friends were. And then I fainted. . . . [loud laughter]. I fainted three more times before I gave in and had sex [loud laughter].

ROHITHA: In the FTZ there are either very, very innocent women or women of the other extreme, like whores. The problem is finding someone in the middle. I mean we don't have to be like Westerners. But we are young and we need to enjoy life.

A MILITARY OFFICER: I cannot blame men for wanting to have sex. It is the women who need to protect their purity.

A NEIGHBOR: There is no value in these women. Their beginning is not good. Think about it, what kind of parent would abandon their young girls in a corrupted place like this for money.

NGO STAFF MEMBER: All this talk of liberation is just talk. Let's be real. Women like this cannot do what women like you do. If their reputation is tarnished what would save them with no jobs after five years, no money, and no husband?

CHATHURI: You should go to the pharmacy and ask for contraceptive pills and check the looks the woman there gives you. It is now much better, because she used to say things or mutter things to the other guy in there. When we are just about to leave she says something like "these are the ones who ruin this country" (culture) or "these things have never happened in our time." Some women yelled at her a couple of years back. Now she only gives funny looks; but the looks say it all.

KUMARI: I wanted him to take me to Mary Strope hospital (to get the abortion done). But he said he didn't have money to go to places in Colombo 7. So we went to this old dilapidated dispensary like place. After the abortion was done, the doctor – although he looked like a fish vendor – told me if I bleed too much to go to the Negombo hospital.

Michel Foucault (1978) famously noted that sexuality exists only because of repressive discourses on sexual practices. The above quotes surely portray a tension-filled field of multiple perspectives, ideologies, and behavioral strategies that reflects layers of gender and social class-based expectations, possibilities, discipline, and violence. All the chapters that follow are intertwined through these parallel and overlapping layers in seeking to elucidate the forbidden zones of global workers' lives.

Chapter 2, entitled " 'Secret' Lives of Good Girls," sets the terms for further discussing how policing and surveillance, particular representational strategies, and ensuing silences shape the sexual subculture in and around the FTZ. It analyzes workers' own understanding of desire and how workers become desiring subjects who nonetheless leave physical desire to be interpreted through ambivalent performances.

Chapter 3, entitled "Romance on the Street," analyzes women workers' varied engagement in sexual banter on city streets to make two major arguments. First, meanings of sexual vocabulary and acts are contextually negotiated, and participating in sexual banter can be empowering for women because it allows them identities outside the dominant mores of respectability. Second, by uncritically adopting Western notions of sexual harassment to condemn banter between working class men and women, many institutions, including NGOs, become guilty of unwittingly promoting docile women who become an ideal assembly-line workforce. The chapter argues that women workers' performances in public spaces convey a specific classed and gendered interpretation of sexual discourse that not only marks their difference from middle-class men and women but constitutes one of the many ways they participate in subaltern politics of citizenship.

Chapter 4, entitled "Would Good Girls Read Such Filth?": Reading and Writing Sex in Katunayake," focuses on women's reading practices: specifically how they read a pornographic magazine in groups in their boarding houses and sometimes send in their own stories for publication. As just about the only forum women have for expressing transgressive desires and activities, this practice enunciates an alternative sexual subculture and does so as a profound challenge to inter-twined discourses on nation, modernity, and female morality. The appearance of two other magazines that espouse an opposing ideology complicated this sce-nario and the chapter explores how both types of magazines offered scripts of sex, romance, and marriage and the roles that go with them – the "bad" modern girl and the "good" modern girl – which the workers readily consume but then use to develop individual notions of love, intimacy, sex, and marriage. The govern-ment prohibited the pornographic magazine in 2006, and the chapter captures the evolving struggle for respectability and good reputation to comment on sexual transgressions, capitalist interests, and how marginalized actors must constantly re-appropriate and reinterpret their resistance.

Chapter 5, entitled "In the Service of the Nation," analyzes how the complex intersections of the political economy of war and transnational production shape FTZ workers' intimate connections to military men and create spaces for violence. I focus on romantic relationships between soldiers of the Sri Lankan armed forces and FTZ workers during the intensified nationalist/militarist discourses during 2000–2009 and the postwar period since May 2009. The war and transnational factory work affected military men and women's social status and respectability in different ways, leading to exploitative relationships. The celebrated war heroes did not mind "undisciplined" factory workers as girlfriends but preferred "disci-plined, good" women who lived with their families as spouses. Caught between broader nationalist expectations of ideal womanly behavior and more subtle con-temporary demands on women's services to war heroes, workers' romances with soldiers often ended in unwanted pregnancies, abortions, and attempted suicide. Workers expressed loyalty to patriotic ideals and gendered national duties while using conscious tactics that reconciled innocent, "good woman" reputations with enjoying romance, sex, and possible marriage to men who might be able to pro-vide a better life than the average village man. Focusing on the new political and economic realities since the civil war ended in May 2009, the chapter evalu-ates how militaristic and capitalistic violence seeps into intimate spaces of now-peaceful areas to comment on militarization's persistent grip on FTZ workers.

Chapter 6, entitled "Guardians of Girls: Policing and Saving Global Workers in Crises of Love and Sex," focuses on gendered and social-class-based responses to what is considered "the crisis of love and sex" within the FTZ area. Based on interviews with police and military officers, boarding house owners, neighbors, factory officials, health service providers, ritual healers, and NGO staff members, this chapter explores how men and women around Katunayake understood their position as guardians and saviors of women workers and responded to situations within their social and moral standing. In several cases, women were disciplined for "moral transgressions" when they had been victims of date rape or statutory rape. Antagonism toward lesbianism was widespread with many expressing frustration that the laws had not changed to punish sexually subversive acts between females. This conflation of laws and morality puts women in a difficult position and forces them to avoid their so called guardians and saviors. This has contributed to a situation where despite various state institutions being established to specifically help workers, women end up relying on local support systems – factory managers, the boarding house sisterhood, landladies, and ritual healers – before seeking help from NGO support services and the police. The resulting violence stemming from not recognizing new sexualities and female sexual desires only forces women to lie and express their desires clandestinely, until the more unfortunate are forced to come out when unwanted pregnancy occurs. The chapter further highlights how the different forms of policing, surveillance, and punishing produces the particular kind of labor needed by late capitalist forms of production.

Chapter 7, entitled "Man-Power Workers, Contract Workers and Tamil Workers: Sexual Empowerment, From Here to Where?," serves as a conclusion and looks ahead to what we can expect in the realms of the sexual. The chapter builds on previous chapters and argues that despite rampant discourses of modernity and globalization, nationalist concerns continue to reign when it comes to evaluating women's behavior. These concerns are expressed not through an overt assault on women's sexually transgressive acts, but by denying them agency and making it difficult for them to express their desires.

Disavowing working women's sexual desires enables the state and its elite to ignore the need for reproductive health services, which is a crude way of disciplining those who dare transgress. By uncritically assuming that all women want to get married after they collect a substantial dowry, elites have colluded with multinational corporations to send women back to their native villages after a few years. This not only allows the factories to recruit new, politically naïve, young, rural women but also provides the families and community members a chance to bring the "undisciplined and corrupt" factory workers back into their fold.

This final chapter further discusses new developments pertaining to the FTZ: recruiting via labor contractors, the increased utilization of part time workers, and the influx of Tamil women workers from the former war torn areas – all of whom now live and work in Katunayake under changing circumstances. After discussing the interesting power dynamics between different groups of female workers, I inquire into how these new workers and their lived worlds clash with established workers and what it might portend for the workers' expressions of desires, pleasures, and intimacies.

All chapters focus on how FTZ women workers recognize the empowering potential of exploring sexual desires despite the attempts made to ensure they remain docile. The book demonstrates how all their decisions, actions, and responses in the sexual realm contribute to the thriving subaltern sexual/political world of the Katunayake FTZ. It thus analyzes the intertwined discourses of global capitalism, nationalism, modernity, and female morality in the context of dominant cultural mores and connects those with ground-level realities of female agency, resistance, and empowerment. After all, as Varunika, a FTZ worker, astutely put it, "Whatever that the monks, or TV or teachers or researchers like you say, we are the ones to live through life and we have to make decisions thinking of our own status (*thathve*). Yes, culture is good, love without sex is good, and to tell you the truth sex is good. But we also are the ones who have to show our mothers in law on the wedding night that we are virgins. So I mean, really, nobody's teachings or advice matter. We have to make decisions taking what is good and best for us at the moment into account. Don't you agree?"

Yes. I do agree!

Notes

1 I only focus on the Katunayake FTZ, the oldest and most important in the country, when exploring the sexual lives and struggles of global factory workers.
2 Bandula Sirimanna, "Sri Lanka Regains US GSP amidst Concerns on Workers' Rights," *Sunday Times* (Business Section), July 12, 2015, p. 9.
3 Interview with the Deputy Director for Industrial Relations. July 2014.
4 Faizal Samath, "Fewer People, More Machines-What's the 'Factory of the Future' Going to Be?" *Sunday Times*, (Business Section), July 12, 2015, p.10.
5 Victor De Munck (1996, 1998) in his writings on romantic love in a Muslim village in Sri Lanka notes that villagers considered sexual desire an integral part of romantic love. However, the very brief notes on this matter do not investigate the linguistic nuances and gendered perceptions associated with love and sex. In the Sinhala language, desire for another (possession of a beautiful woman or a wealthy man) and desire for sex, often can be two different things. However, more often than not the same terms, such as *ashawa* or *thanhawa*, are used to describe both. Villagers in Kutali spoke Tamil as opposed to the Sinhala speaking people I studied, but without more ethnographic details and analyzes it is difficult to know if a woman desiring a man sexually is no different to a man desiring a woman. A woman desiring a man because of love or the need for security via marriage, however, is not vilified, even if such desire is not always allowed to be fulfilled.
6 Presumably India's premier nation-making narrative, the Ramayana and its many interpretations not only shaped the country's anti-colonial struggle but has also influenced its post-independence trajectories.
7 Jordal et al. (2014) note that unmarried migrant workers' concern for respectability and virginity poses serious implications for their sexual and reproductive health and rights.

References

Ahearn, L. (2003) Writing Desire in Nepali Love Letters. *Language and Communication.* 23 (2). pp. 107–122.
Arondekar, A. (2009) *For the Record: On Sexuality and the Colonial Archive in India.* Durham, NC: Duke University Press.
Bose, B. (2008) Modernity, Globality, Sexuality, and the City: A Reading of Indian Cinema. *The Global South.* 2 (1). pp. 35–58.
Brow, J. (1999) Utopia's New-Found Space: Images of the Village Community in the Early Writings of Ananda Kumaraswamy. *Modern Asian Studies.* 33 (1). pp. 67–86.

Butler, J. (2009) AIBR. Revista de Antropología Iberoamericana. www.aibr.org Volumen 4, Número 3: i–xiii. Madrid: Antropólogos Iberoamericanos en.

Caldeira, T. (1999) Fortified Enclaves: The New Urban Segregation. In Low, S. (ed.). *Theorizing the City: The New Anthropology Reader*. New Brunswick: Rutgers University Press. pp. 83–110.

Chapin, Bambi. (2014) Childhood in a Sri Lankan Village. New Brunswick, N.J: Rutgers University Press.

Chatterjee, P. (1993) *The Nation and Its Fragments: Colonial and Post Colonial Histories*. Princeton: Princeton University Press.

Dabindu Collective. (1997) *A Review of Free Trade Zones in Sri Lanka*. Boralesgamuwa: CRC Press.

De Alwis, M. (1997) The Production and Embodiment of Respectability: Gendered Demeanors in Colonial Ceylon. In Roberts, M. (ed.). *Sri Lanka Collective Identities Revisited*. Colombo: Marga Institute. pp. 105–144.

Deleuze, G. and Guattari, F. (1983) *A Thousand Plateaus: Capitalism and Schizophrenia*. Minneapolis: University of Minnesota Press.

De Munck, Victor. (1996) Love and Marriage in a Sri Lankan Muslim Community: Toward a Reevaluation of Dravidian Marriage Practices. *American Ethnologist*. 23 (4). pp. 698–716.

De Munck, Victor. (1998). Lust, Love and Arranged Marriages in Sri Lanka. In De Munck, Victor (ed.). *Romantic Love and Sexual Behavior: Perspectives from the Social Sciences*. Connecticut: Praegar. pp. 285–300.

Domosh, Mona. (1998) "Those Gorgeous Incongruities": Polite Politics and Public Space on the Streets of Nineteenth Century New York City. *Annals of the Association of American Geographers*. 88 (2). pp. 209–226.

Enstad, N. (1999) *Ladies of Labor, Girls of Adventure: Working Women, Popular Culture and Labor Politics at the Turn of the Twentieth Century*. New York: Columbia University Press.

Fernandez-Kelly, M.P. (1983) *For We are Sold, I and My People*. Albany: SUNY Press.

Freeman, C. (2000) *High Tech and High Heels in the Global Economy: Women, Work, and Pink-Collar Identities in the Caribbean*. Durham: Duke University Press.

Foucault, M. (1978) *The History of Sexuality*, Volume 1. New York: Vintage.

Greenberg, D. (1995) The Pleasures of Homosexuality. In Abramson, P. and Pinkerton, S. (eds.). *Sexual Nature, Sexual Culture*. Chicago: University of Chicago Press. pp. 223–256.

Gunawardana, S. (2010) What does Transnational Solidarity Mean for Sri Lanka's Migrant Women Workers? In Bieler, A. and Lindberg, I. (eds.). *Transnational Solidarity in Times of Global Restructuring: Prospects for New Alliances across Borders*. London: Routledge. pp. 87–100.

Guruge, A. (1965) *Anagarika Dharmapala: Return to Righteousness*. Colombo: Government Press.

Hewamanne, S. (2008a) *Stitching Identities in a Free Trade Zone: Gender and Politics in Sri Lanka*. Philadelphia: University of Pennsylvania Press.

Hewamanne, S. (2008b) "City of Whores": Nationalism, Development and Global Garment Workers of Sri Lanka. *Social Text*. 95 (2). pp. 35–59.

Hewamanne, S. (2012) Negotiating Sexual Meanings: Global Discourses, Local Practices and Free Trade Zone Workers on City Streets. *Ethnography*. 13 (3). pp. 352–374.

Jordal, Malin, Wijewardena, Kumudu, Ohman, Ann, Essen Brigitta, and Olsson, Pia. (2014) Negotiating Respectability: Migrant Women Workers' Perceptions of Relationships and Sexuality in Free Trade Zones in Sri Lanka. *Health Care for Women International*. 35. pp. 658–676.

Lorde, A. (2007) Uses of the Erotic: The Erotic as Power. In *Sister Outsider: Essays and Speeches by Audrey Lorde*. Berkeley: Crossing Press. pp. 53–59.

Low, S. (2001) The Edge and the Center: Gated Communities and the Discourse of Urban Fear. *American Anthropologist*. 103 (1). pp. 45–58.

Manderson, L. and Aggleton, P. (2003) Belief Systems and the Place of Desire: Perspectives from Asia and the Pacific. Editorial Introduction. *Culture, Health & Sexuality*. 5 (3). pp. 181–184.

Mills, M.B. (1999) *Thai Women in the Global Labor Force: Consuming Desires: Contested Selves*. New Brunswick: Rutgers University Press.

Moore, M. (1985) *The State and Peasant Politics in Sri Lanka*. Cambridge: Cambridge University Press.

Murray, D. (1999) Laws of Desire? Race, Sexuality and Power in Male Martinican Sexual Narratives. *American Ethnologist*. 26 (1). pp. 160–172.

Obeyesekere, G. (1984) *The Cult of the Goddess Pattini*. Chicago: University of Chicago Press.

Peiss, K. (1986) *Cheap Amusements: Working Women and Leisure in Turn of the Century New York*. Philadelphia: Temple University Press.

Pena, D. (1997) *The Terror of the Machine: Technology, Work, Gender and Ecology on the U.S.-Mexico Border*. Austin: University of Texas.

Pun, N. (2005) *Made in China: Women Factory Workers in a Global Workplace*. Durham: Duke University Press.

Ruwanpura, E. (2011) Sex or Sensibility? The Making of Chaste Women and Promiscuous Men in a Sri Lankan University Setting (*The University of Edinburgh*, 2011–11–22).

Salzinger, L. (2003) *Genders in Production: Making Workers in Mexico's Global Factories*. Berkley: University of California Press.

Shah, S. (2014) *Street Corner Secrets: Sex, Work, and Migration in the City of Mumbai*. Durham: Duke University Press.

Smart, A. (2001) Unruly Places: Urban Governance and the Persistence of Illegality in Hong Kong's Urban Squatter Areas. *American Anthropologist*. 103 (1). pp. 30–44.

Smith, M. (2010) Erasure of Sexuality and Desire: State Morality and Sri Lankan Migrants in Beirut, Lebanon. *The Asia Pacific Journal of Anthropology*. 11 (3–4). pp. 378–393.

Srivastava, S. (ed.) (2004) *Sexual Sites, Seminal Attitudes: Sexualities, Masculinities and Culture in South Asia*. London: Sage.

Vanita, R. (ed.) (2002) *Queering India: Same Sex Love and Eroticism in Indian Culture and Society*. New York: Routledge.

Wolf, D. (1992) *Factory Daughters: Gender, Household Dynamics and Rural Industrialization in Java*. Berkeley: University of California Press.

Yuval-Davis, N. (1997) *Gender and Nation*. London: Sage.

Yuval-Davis, N. (2012) *The Politics of Belonging: Intersectional Contestations*. London: Sage.

Zacharias, U. (2001) Trial by Fire: Gender, Power and Citizenship in Narratives of the Nation. *Social Text*. 19 (4). pp. 29–51.

2 "Secret" lives of good girls

On romances, sexualities, and unuttered desires

The 2002 movie *Sulang Kirrilli* [*Wind Bird*] by Inoka Sathyangani explored a relationship between a global factory worker and an army soldier. The movie depicts both man and woman happily engaging in physical intimacy. When the worker finds herself pregnant, she starts dreaming of a secure married life with the soldier. But she is brought back to reality when the man asks her to get an abortion and she finds out that he is married with children. The movie cleverly portrays how the worker moves back and forth between a dream world – where the man comes back for her and marries her – and reality, where she is reviled for having engaged in premarital sex.

A movie that came out in 2000 and was directed by H. D. Premaratne, titled *Kinihiriya Mal* (*Flowers under the Anvil*), also focused on the life of a poor village woman who migrates to work in the FTZ and the repercussions stemming from her desire for wealth and things material. Sanduni, who is quickly attracted to the consumer culture in the FTZ, becomes an easy victim of city vices. Due to her incessant desire for new, shiny accoutrements and a modern life style, she leaves her FTZ job and becomes a masseur at a city massage parlor. However, retribution for her "*thanhawa*" (desire for money) follows Sanduni and her family when her village gets to know of her occupation. The incensed villagers stone her family home, leading to the deaths of her father and brother. Incidentally, another FTZ worker from the village, who avoids being swayed by the new attractions in the city and chooses poverty over "quick money," gets applauded. Media promotions heralded the movie as "a story of a seamstress of our time."[1]

While both movies addressed issues relevant to my work, they focused on individual stories and did not cover the complex web of social, economic, and cultural relations within which global factory workers make decisions about their intimate lives, finances, and ways to attain modern life styles. The movies were especially silent about the circumstances under which migrant FTZ workers developed sexual desires and how they themselves understood and experienced desires. This chapter seeks to illuminate the women's quest for sexual agency and how the existing conditions complicate their lives.

Focusing on migrant global workers in the city does not mean that village women are devoid of sexual desires. The sexual urges these women experience are no different from what all women experience. What is different is how their sexuality is understood and expressed. The cultural expectation that sexual inno-cence ought to be maintained until marriage causes Sinhala women (and men) to control their sexual urges, which in turn cause them to explain away erotic longings and transgressions by resorting to culturally understood mechanisms like trances and other supernatural influences. The FTZ, however, allows them to experience a space away from kin and village surveillance, making it more condu-cive to explore, experience, and interpret sexual desires, intimacies, and relations.

The process of FTZ women workers becoming desiring subjects who are able to more openly express desires is intimately connected to the process of construct-ing new senses of self and building an identity as a gendered group of migrant industrial workers. Investing their immediate life spaces and social practices with meaning and using subcultural styles and aesthetics are crucial to creating and sustaining individual and group identities (Willis 1993; Kondo 1997; Hewamanne 2008). Global factory workers at the Katunayake FTZ collectively create different tastes and cultural practices by rejecting, appropriating, and mixing and match-ing parts of cultural systems available to them. These new tastes and sensibili-ties in music, dance, film, reading matter, styles of dress, and body mannerisms expressed and registered a different identity for themselves as a gendered migrant group of industrial workers, who are different from men, middle class women, and non-migrant industrial workers (Hewamanne 2003, 2008a).

Intertwined with these new tastes and preferences, which they called becoming modernized or "mod," was an urgent need to start and enjoy romantic relation-ships with their subversions in beauty, fashion, and demeanor partly designed toward creating intimacy with working class males. It was almost as if becoming an experienced urban, global factory worker required one to not just adopt new tastes and practices but also be bold enough to roam the nearby areas hand in hand with one's boyfriend. Just as their new tastes did not go unchallenged, their "craze to find boyfriends and squeeze into corners," as one neighbor told me, did not go undisputed.

This chapter shows how physical desire is unuttered and is often interpreted through ambivalent performances. Women perceived and expressed their own physical desires within a specific social, cultural context and used language spe-cific to that culture. The following material will traverse through this fluid field of communication to unravel how women workers themselves understand and experience desire. The chapter sets the terms for the discussion concerning varied practices, acts, and policing and surveillance of various actors in response to the FTZ's sexual subculture that follows.

As women migrate from rural agricultural communities to the FTZs, they encounter new global cultural flows and acquire new knowledges leading to new senses of selves. These new senses of self, however, co-exist with deeply internal-ized notions of what it means to be an ideal Sinhala Buddhist rural woman. The articulation of these apparently incompatible positions of being urban industrial workers and young unmarried daughters from patriarchal villages enable viable spaces for creativity, tactics, and strategies. In the following discussion I ana-lyze the way FTZ workers desired, learned, engaged, and performed intimate relationships and how this is connected to their FTZ identities, which gets registered through certain practices and symbolic functions of the body via its adornment and accessories (words, gestures). The love and sex Sujani, Geethi, and Nadi experienced are representative of many FTZ worker romantic relationships.

Sujani

"I can't wait to fall in love with a good man and enjoy life in the FTZ," Sujani, a 17-year-old new FTZ worker, gushed. "I want to attend all the night musical shows and go on as many trips as I can. If I have a boyfriend I can say that I have weekend work and then go places with him. I feel sad when I see couples walk in hand in hand. I think to myself 'they are going to the movies or to the beaches. How good would it be if I can do that too?'" On other occasions, Sujani said she would like to experience being kissed. She had yet to enjoy her first kiss. "My village boyfriend and I never got a chance to be alone. We held hands many times and once he touched my face while walking to the temple. I want to know how it is to be kissed."

According to Sujani, there were no real barriers to falling in love with a boy in the village. "But then as soon as the parents found out they either need to get married or forget about the relationship. And there is not even a movie theater in our village. There is one in Polonnaruwa, but that is about ten miles from my village. It is rarely I saw a movie before coming here," she complained. However, she said that it was not considered a bad thing to go to the movies as long as women went with other women and family members. "But if you get caught going to a movie with a man, then your future is destroyed. The whole family would be disgraced. Once a letter from a boy was found inside a girl's text book in our school and she was publicly berated and was almost expelled. So we had to be very careful if we wanted to have a boyfriend. Now you saw what happened to me. They stopped my schooling and sent me here. I was underage. They forged my birth certificate so that I can work here. All because of one silly boyfriend," Sujani laughed with a wicked glint in her eye knowing that her parents unwittingly ended up providing her a better environment to enjoy life.

In contrast to her time in the village, Sujani had seen several movies since coming to the FTZ. She had also gone on a day trip to a temple and went to the fair almost every Sunday. "Just walking back from work I see many things and I learn many things. Everything around here is colorful. In the village it is always green and brown. It is rarely that we saw yellow, pink or blue," she said while wrinkling her face so as to show how dull her life in the village had been. "Why, do you think the sky is of a different color in our village," Shamila asked Sujani with a laugh. "It was blue alright, but how often did we notice it. We were like frogs in the well. We had only the village so we liked the village," Sujani retorted. Soon Sujani wrote to her village boyfriend to come to Katunayake so they could enjoy life. He came once and then wrote her an admonishing letter asking her to refrain from taking pleasure trips and to behave herself by observing good manners.

This did not sit well with Sujani who was quickly acquiring all the clothing and fashion accessories needed to be a "mod" garment girl and was already attracting many a man's eye. Predictably, she broke off with her village boyfriend within six months of coming to the FTZ and started a romantic relationship with an army soldier who had deserted his position at the front lines. This gave her the opportunity to indulge in all that she had dreamt of: going to movies, musical shows, pleasure trips, and even shopping. Talking about her own sister who refused to have a boyfriend, Sujani said, "What's the point in having pretty dresses and costume jewelry if you don't have a boyfriend to go places with. Yes, we can go places with other girls, but you feel left out or like a burden to them when other girls come with their boyfriends."

Sujani once talked to me about sexual pleasures and said she had not given in when her boyfriend encouraged her to engage in sex and did not intend to do so before marriage. She said the best part of the relationship with her army boyfriend was that she felt complete and whole and could do things with him that she could not by herself, such as going to the beach, movies, and beautiful faraway places. She also said that because of him she had something to talk and boast about when with friends. Due to her young age at the time, Sujani directly associated romantic relationships with companionship and to her journey toward becoming a street-wise "mod" FTZ worker. Other narratives on relationships also somewhat less explicitly showed that women partly view boyfriends as a resource, in the sense that men could accompany and guide them when discovering city life. Geethi's narrative, however, focused more prominently on sexual desires or the lack thereof.

Geethi

"The first day I came here both my mother and father came with me. Before they left me at the boarding house they advised me a lot and asked me to protect my good name and the honor of my family. They cried a lot and I cried too. I was just so sad and I promised myself I will never do anything to shame them and that I would never abandon my rural values (*gamekama*). *Ane*, Sandya miss, I myself can't even believe how fast I forgot all that and became just like any other FTZ girl," Geethi, a six-year veteran FTZ worker at the time of the interview, laughed as she recalled her entry into the FTZ. She continued, "I just loved everything about Katunayake. I loved working in the factory. I liked all my new friends. Just walking to work and back one learns a lot. Those days everything looked rosy to me. I felt adventurous, as if I was finally living life and not just looking at it. The other residents in my boarding house never left me alone. They included me in everything they did. I liked to spend time with them at the boarding house. Those days I just counted my fingers to the day I got my salary. The first thing I did was to go shopping and buy things that all the other girls here seemed to own, you know, dresses, shoes, colorful hair braids, perfumes, and, of course, gold rings. But after about one year of this buying frenzy I started feeling like I was one of the 'in crowd' at the FTZ. Then I started helping my parents more. Now that I have been working here for six years I have all my jewelry and I also bought some furniture for my dowry." Then she lowered her voice and added, "I have had four boy friends over these past six years. I can tell you this because you are like a sister to me and you have gone to different countries and know the world. I even slept with three of those boyfriends."

The next day early in the afternoon we sat under the mango tree by the well and I asked her whether she could tell me more about these relationships. It was a hot Sunday and nobody, except for the woman sweeping the garden with her back to us, was within hearing distance. Geethi hesitated and then sought my right hand and squeezed it tightly. She did not let go of my hand till she finished telling me about all four of her boyfriends. "I was crazily in love with my first boyfriend," she said with a dreamy smile. "I mean, those first few months I thought that I was in heaven. I loved it when he kissed and touched me. So when he asked me to go to a rooming house I went willingly and I also did not object to having sex. I just hated the whole sex experience. It was so painful and I was sick with fever for five days. After that I did not even want to look at his face again. But I do not blame him for what happened in the room. I can tell you miss that maybe in my own heart I wanted to experience sex. I mean kissing and hugging were great. And you know how one leads to the other. But oh, Sandya miss, were my eyes opened or what? It was a bad, bad experience. And then I was without a boyfriend for about three months. But I felt lonely and felt as if I was missing out on life. So I found another boyfriend. I did not like him much and did not even like the way he looked. But we were o.k., in fact we were happy for a while. Then surprise, surprise, he wanted to have sex. And I was thinking, well, what is there to lose now. The hymen (*kanya patalaya*) is already gone and there is nothing for me to protect now. So we had sex. *Apoi*, this time too it was painful. He felt it too and soon he abandoned me. Not that I cared. I was relieved," Geethi laughed and stood up while still holding my hand and forcing me to stand up with her. Two women had moved close to the well and appeared to want to eavesdrop on our conversation even as they kept soaking their laundry in big basins.

Still holding my hand, Geethi started walking toward the railroad. "I tell these things to you because you are an educated woman. You can understand why sometimes we do things that we are not supposed to do. I don't want everyone to know these details," she said while taking a quick glance at the two intruders. "Now the third boyfriend was younger than me and he came from a very remote village. That boy treated me with lots of respect and love. We went to many places together and were very happy. *Ane*, look at how bad my *karma* is; because as soon as I started thinking about marrying him some people told him about my old boyfriends and soon that relationship also ended."

Disillusioned with finding love again, Geethi lived alone for about one year and still enjoyed going on trips, shopping, and engaging in other fun activities in the area with her girlfriends. Some rumors had reached her village through another FTZ worker from the area, but since there were so many rumors about all the workers at the FTZ this did not make much difference. "Besides, the way I acted at home, like everybody's innocent little girl, nobody really could believe such things about me," Geethi said. "About a year ago a boarding friend's cousin came after me saying that he would forget all my past misdeeds." My friend cautioned me about this man but I thought that since there is nothing more for me to lose I would just enjoy the relationship. From the very first day we started sleeping together. Now for the good part: I finally started liking sex. I don't know whether that is the reason, but I fell in love with him. But then he left me for another woman and I cried for days. I vowed that I would never have a boyfriend again. I have been in this area for a long time now. I don't need a man to go places any-more. You must have already noticed that it is I who organize groups of women to go to musical shows and on other trips. I am an old hand here now." She again laughed lightheartedly, and I made a mental note of the fact that Geethi did not say that men forced her to have sex or that she felt guilty or impure due to having had premarital sex – a claim many women resorted when explaining their experience with premarital sex.

Kishali

"I had a line of boyfriends since coming to the FTZ, and I wanted to marry all of them. But it was my bad karma that all these boyfriends were opportunistic crooks," Kishali, a 36-year-old, unmarried FTZ worker, said. She further added that as soon as she started a relationship something made her trust the men com-pletely and that she spent her hard earned money on buying them gifts and pro-viding other financial help. At the time of the interview, she was in the process of fighting to win back her last boyfriend who, she learned, had maintained relation-ships with two other women while dating her. "One day I met up with his second girlfriend to sort things out and we found him with a third woman. All three of us beat him with our umbrellas until they broke," she said while laughing. Just as nonchalantly she continued, "now I am seeing sorcerers and magicians to get him away from these other two women."

Patterns of romances

Interview excerpts from these three workers capture some common patterns among FTZ workers' love and sexual lives. The 17-year-old new worker wanted to enjoy and experiment with intimate relationships, while the other two, hav-ing spent several years at the FTZ, experienced several relationships. They recognized how they conflated notions of love and intimacy with instrumental desires, such as wanting protection, security, and practical companionship. Just like these two latter women, most FTZ workers I met sincerely wanted to marry their first boyfriend and subsequent ones, even though they were not very clear about their feelings for these men. In most cases, men abandoned the women after a few months of dalliance to pursue other women (often after taking finan-cial and sexual advantage). When women themselves left a man, most times it was because they got to know that the man had other girlfriends or was already married.

All the workers I interviewed formally and associated with over the years said that the taboos associated with premarital sex, the threat of social ostracization and the potential for unwanted pregnancies were why they did not want to engage in premarital sex. Yet only a few were able to resist sexual demands, and this was mainly because many felt that satisfying their men was the best way to keep the men from abandoning them. This resulted in stories of anxiety-filled and sometimes even physically painful sexual experiences, at least initially.

Seya, one of the women with whom I conducted life history interviews, somewhat lightheartedly said, "The first time when the sex was happening, in my mind, I envisioned getting on to the *poruwa* (the ceremonial platform where marriage rituals are conducted), fainting, as is supposed to happened to women who lose virginity before marriage, and getting beaten by the elders of both sides for shaming them." But then, she confessed to feeling as if an enormous weight had lifted from her shoulders – the burden of protecting her virginity – and she started gradually enjoying sex. "That is, until I became pregnant and he ran away."

Given social conventions pertaining to premarital sex, women who have had sex and lost their virginity become dependent on men in the hopes that they will ultimately marry them, which then leads to their being exploited financially and for domestic service. The men in general fully subscribe to the stigma attached to women living away from their parents and therefore do not consider the workers worthy partners for marriage, which makes it easy for them to abandon the women after the first or first few sexual encounters. Consequently, verbal battles and physical struggles among lovers, of the kind Kishali described above, are common around Katunayake's public spaces. Stories of women using magic to keep a wandering boyfriend with her or to take revenge on lovers who jilted them abound. The tell-tale signs of numerous magicians, sorcerers, palm and horoscope readers' offices are easy to find around the FTZ. In such circumstances, relationships such as Nadee's were rare and were what many aspired to attain.

Nadee

Women considered having a boyfriend who did not want premarital sex and wished to get married soon as the ideal situation. Women who were able to maintain a relationship without engaging in sex were branded the "talented ones (*daksha*)." Nadee's relationship aptly illustrates the ideal. She was from Anamaduwa and worked at the UTP factory cleaning tobacco. A short time after she started working in the FTZ she found a boyfriend and they spent almost all their off days together going to places like parks, temples, and shopping malls in Colombo. "He would like to marry me even tomorrow if I so desire. I just want to have a bit more fun before getting married," she said and added, "It is only a clever girl who can keep a man loyal. It needs much maneuvering. Pride, submission, fights, and tears all help. You can control a man on tears alone."

Nadee also talked about Shamila, who lived in the same boarding house as herself, saying, "I don't know about Neela, but Shamila just does not know how to keep a man interested." "Neela had once told another girl that Ajith is in so much love with me because I give him everything he asks for. I don't care for such jealous talk. I can leave him just this minute and will be as pure as I was when I came here from my village." Neela, however, thought otherwise and said, "You know why Nadee is trying to go to a Middle Eastern country? So that she can earn money to cover what she lacks [virginity]. Can any number of gold sovereigns cover that lack?" Neela seemed to compensate for her inability to achieve the "ideal romantic relationship" by undermining Nadee's achievement. Voluntarily explaining why she did not have a boyfriend, Neela said, "even if Nadee has not done the big thing [sexual intercourse] any relationship involves some hanky-panky.[2] Boys do not want good women like us who do not like such things." Neela later elaborated that there were many ways to have sex without damaging the hymen. "One is, you know, the hand job. There is another thing that men call "stone cutting" or "lapidary," [inter-femoral sex]" she explained in a hushed tone.

Nadee's relationship exemplified the kind of relationship that many women workers desired. Although Nadee's romance was squarely within patriarchal contours of what a relationship ought to be, many workers desired that. Yet, men's attitude, stigma surrounding FTZ work, lack of knowledge and access to contraceptives made achieving this a difficult task.

Pleasures, violence, and desire for love

Many workers, even those who exclusively blamed women for having sex, thought it was a crime if a man abandoned a woman after having sex with her for the first time. They used the term *anatha wuna* (became worthless) to describe losing one's virginity. Many women thought that men attempted to tempt them into having sex to test their virtue. As Geethi explained, "If you are tempted (if you show signs of arousal and give in), then they consider such women as easy and too desirous (*wal*) and do not think they are good enough to marry. Well, if you do not do what they ask, then they in any case leave you because of sexual frustration. So we cannot win, might as well enjoy what we can."

During my formal interviews, friendly conversations, and observations of their interactions with boyfriends, it became clear how women's understanding of desire and violence (social, emotional, and even physical) are loosely intertwined. Many workers thought that unmarried women were unlikely to find sex pleasurable because they were likely to be pressured into the act or did so while fearing its consequences. Mela, while laughing, went through the motions (performing) how a woman would be looking up at the fan and thinking "Will he leave me, or not" (*mu mawa dala yaida, nadda*) while in the middle of intercourse. Many also thought that FTZ relationships rarely took place without emotional or physical violence. In fact, relationship-related violence around the FTZ area is high and neighbors and police also considered such incidents "normal."

At Saman's boarding house, where I sometimes stayed, and frequently visited during my long term fieldwork, I saw much violence within relationships, the kind that must have prompted the workers' understanding of relationship dynamics.

Saman's girlfriend Chuti cooked and cleaned for him and yet he seemed to pay her back by verbally and physically abusing her. Chuti's eldest sister was the one who first found a FTZ job. She stayed at Saman's boarding house and eventually became his girlfriend. When the middle sister came to the boarding house Saman started sleeping with both of them. When Chuti moved in, according to other residents, he visited all three of them in the same room. After a few months of this, a senior resident intervened and the sisters' mother came to negotiate with Saman. Soon the older two sisters moved to a different boarding house, in the hope that Saman would marry Chuti. Saman, however, physically abused Chuti at least once a week, yet a few hours later he cooked, cleaned, and even did laundry for her as a way of atoning for his behavior. During the year I spent staying at and visiting the boarding house, there were four couples and the men in these relationships regularly beat the female partner. There was a woman who had two abortions (having had her first one before this) during my stint at the boarding house. We also heard of many other beatings and abortions taking place among residents in surrounding boarding houses.

Although no worker explicitly said that domestic violence was justifiable or alright or that they would accept violence in their relationships, such an environment where violence was considered normal made them tolerate intimate partner abuse in their own relationships. As Deepika once told me, "Violence-free relationships are only for women who have done many meritorious deeds in their last birth (*pin karapu* ayata). That's why they are born into big families." Deepika's boyfriend (who later married her) did not physically abuse her but used rough language whenever it suited him. Deepika said she is appreciative that he is not physically abusive, and thought that even if he starts being physically abusive she would give him several chances before leaving him. "The situation here is very different Sandya akke," She explained. "Men are brought up to think that if physical abuse is not excessive then it is fine for men to punish their women in that way. We (women) are brought up to think that it is alright too. And then all the relationships around here seem to be abusive. I cannot be special. I have to contemplate all the other benefits of having a boyfriend or being married, over occasional physical abuse. Without our economic situation changing, none of this will change." As Deepika so astutely noted, many women understood the connection between their social class positioning and the particular dynamics of their relationships. Despite knowing that relationships could portend violence and misery, they still desired to be in one and in many cases willingly or unwillingly engaged in premarital sex.

Desires, denials, and locally specific expressions

Although women workers desired romantic relationships, many I talked to disavowed having sexual desires or seeking sexual satisfaction through these relationships. Even when they agreed that they had experienced sexual relations, women said it was the men's insistence that led to it. In 2000, Geethi was the only woman who explicitly acknowledged that she herself desired sex.

By 2015 Sri Lankan society had undergone major changes. It was six years since the nearly three decade long civil war had ended, the authoritarian Mahinda Rajapaksa government had been ousted, there was access to cable television almost everywhere, and internet services were available via mobile phones. Revealing clothes, dating, and partying have become common among Colombo youth. Many speculated that young people in universities and high schools (especially international schools) engaged in premarital sex.[3] While people were still reluctant to approve of premarital sex or even dating before a certain age, urban youth are much more open and accepting of such activities. My interviews in 2015, however, showed that these urban trends did not have much impact on FTZ workers in general. They continued to deny having sexual desires and claimed they would avoid premarital sex if that was possible. Just as in 2000, many easily and eagerly discussed other workers' sexual activities while maintaining ambivalent opinions on premarital sex.

This denial of sexual desires was not surprising, given that society in general still looks down, ostracizes, and discriminates against women who evidence erotic or lustful behavior. However, when premarital sex, unwanted pregnancies, and abortions were discovered, women who claimed they had been pressured for sex by their boyfriends elicited sympathy and practical support. This, some workers claimed, was why many girlfriends deny their role in sexual activities and conveniently place all blame on men.

Another strategy that some women resorted to, especially during the late 1990s and 2009 (when the war ended), was to claim that the boyfriend was a military man stationed at the front lines and that the sex resulted from a sense of duty toward these national war heroes. In the same vein, when men abandoned pregnant women, the latter claimed that the soldier boyfriend was killed in battle before they could get married as planned. Both claims elicited sympathetic responses from their fellow workers and even neighbors.

As Eshani Ruwanpura noted with regard to female university students, many of whom are also from rural working class families, their aspirations to use education and marriage for upward social mobility constrain their sexualities and lead to rules and systems of surveillance that they impose on themselves and others (2011). FTZ workers also aspired to a better life, even if it was not at the same level female university students did, and they too created rules and norms and resorted to secrecy when dealing with sexual behavior.

After reading and re-reading interview and participant observation material, which showed contradictions between women's expressed opinions and their acts, I started questioning whether it is I, now steeped in Western ways of thinking about sexuality and desire, who was not seeing or was misreading their expressions. In 2014 I conducted an object feedback interview in which I played a popular Sinhala song to some women workers and had them discuss it. Although I started the exercise with 15 workers, 23 women workers ultimately participated in the discussion. I only present here selected portions from what was an especially thought provoking, and at times, heated discussion.

The song was written by Mahinda Chandrasekera and sung by Nirosha Virajini. What follows is a crude translation, as many similes and metaphors defy translation.

> Does the full moon come tearing through the darkness in the chena
> to kiss the golden wheat flowers?
>
> What is the point in waiting at home dreaming all night?
> Beautiful man (*rankanda*) are you still up
> Protecting the chena (from wild animals)?
>
> Does the full moon come tearing through the darkness in the chena
> to kiss the golden wheat flowers?
>
> I feel like lying down on the verandah
> Under the sky where blue stars are winking at me
> Parrots do not come to eat mangoes tomorrow
> Although the flowers blossom, the tree still does not have fruits
>
> Does the full moon come tearing through the darkness in the chena
> to kiss the golden wheat flowers?
>
> I only have merits enough to dream about the golden flower bed,
> where my meritorious elephant (handsome man) sleeps like a golden pillar
>
> Does the full moon come tearing through the darkness in the chena
> to kiss the golden wheat flowers?
>
> How are we going to become a group of three?
> Isn't there enough room in my bed for a little golden son?

I asked each in the original group of 15 to write what they thought the woman was singing about. They did not have to write their names on the paper. Thirteen women noted that the singer is lamenting the loneliness (using one or more of three Sinhala words: *paluwa, kansiya,* and *thanikama*) that she feels because her husband is away at night protecting their chena. Six of them noted that this is a newly married woman, but did not note that she is longing for sexual pleasure with her husband. All 15 said the woman is longing for a baby and lamenting that economic hardships are forcing her husband to work at night and preventing her from conceiving. One woman among the two women who did not mention loneliness said that the woman is singing about her husband's impotence (*bari-kama*) and how this is causing her to be childless. The remaining women simply described the similes and metaphors without giving an opinion.

The woman who mentioned impotence argued her case well. But the other women noted that she is praising her husband using words such as *rankanda* (golden body) and *pinsara mage athu* (my meritorious elephant) and that a woman who is unhappy with a man's sexual prowess would not have used such words. Most of them were adamant that she misses her husband's company. When I highlighted several lines alluding to wanting a baby, they agreed that it was a major theme of the song. Still no one suggested the woman was longing for sexual pleasure. When I pointed out that the woman's need for a baby may be a surreptitious cry for sex, Kavita said, "She is in fact singing to her in laws saying that he is away and, therefore, don't expect me to have babies." This elicited laughter, but many workers present variously agreed with this by saying that mothers-in-law want babies as soon as people get married and usually blame the woman for not conceiving.

After more prodding the workers agreed that there is a subtle allusion to missing her husband's company, but they also noted that this may or may not be sexual. Even after I pointed out that the song was written by a man, they claimed that a good lyricist would know how rural women think and would not write about a woman crying seeking sexual gratification. All throughout this discussion the woman who thought the song is about the husband's impotence disagreed with everybody and argued that the song is about her sadness and that perhaps she is singing with the hope that someone would help her conceive. Even then she only talked about the desire to conceive and not about wanting sexual intercourse.

I presented another song sung by Nanda Mailini and written by Professor Sunil Ariyaratne to the same group of women. The song translates as follows:

> Leader among the shepherds (Govindu/Krishna),
> in this beautiful bed I am like a she bear who has lost her cubs.
> Even the river Yamuna is shaken
> thinking about our former beautiful sexual games . . . (*rathikelli ramani*)
> Moon rays enter from fissures among the tree covers like arrows that burn the heart. Wounded by the king of physical desire (*mada rada*)
> the youthful body does not allow any rest.
> This is a night other lovers become tired
> but Radha is shaken by the separation.

The song is written in scholarly and metaphoric Sinhala and Sanskrit, perhaps a prudent ploy considering that the song would have been banned if it was written in everyday Sinhala language. Though this song conveyed a message close to many workers' hearts, none of the women were able to decipher the erotic content. They liked the tune and said that since it is a Nanda Malini song it must be a good song with deep meaning. When I explained each metaphor, there was much laughter and witty rejoinders, with some saying "This woman has such poison/pain (*harima visayak* and *mara gayak*)." But several remembered the Radha/Krishna story, and how theirs was a higher form of love and connection and that they were deities dancing in a forest with no one around. Chamila made all of us laugh by saying, "Wow, this song is super . . . it contained obscenities (*kunuharupa*) right in the middle and we had no idea." However, many said that this is about India and divine love, and that they do not feel it has anything to do with their lives.

When at a different focus group I discussed certain words and participants agreed that desire (*ashawa, thanhawa*) has to do with wanting and attachment. It could pertain to wealth or family as well as good food, alcohol, and sex. They variously noted terms for overtly expressed arousal, such as *kulappu wela, mada kipila* (both terms associated with elephants in heat), and *madana mathe* (sexual craziness). They struggled to provide a term that described a non-expressed desire for sexual intercourse. They again noted *paaluwa, kansiya,* and *thanikama* in different combinations to express how they sometimes longed to see their boyfriends. The words provided to describe female sexiness were *dangale thiyena, vise kariyek, nattichchiyek, manamala pata,* and *val pata.* These words defy good translation, but an approximate translation would be physicality, one with the poison, female dancer, bridal look, and wild look, respectively.

Later, while analyzing this data, I was struck by how often workers associated relationships with loneliness (*paaluwa, kansiya, thanikama*). It also figured in their narration of how men tried to pressure them into sex. A study of FTZ area men I conducted for another research project evidenced that men also liberally use the Sinhala words for loneliness to describe their sexual encounters. This made me question whether sexual desire gets expressed in culturally specific codes, such as "unbearable loneliness." That is until women have to openly admit or deny sexual desire, which happens when sex leads to crises such as pregnancy.

At the end of one of my visits to Katunayake, Gayani gave me a hand-decorated card that enclosed a poem she had written about me. The poem was written by changing the words of a popular Sinhala song and read

> You are a tear drop,
> warmly felt
> comforting to the mind;
> Like a tear that falls from a mother's eyes
> Does that tear drop have a name or a village on it?

At the end of each visit, it is common for the current and former FTZ workers I spend time with to give me small gifts, handmade cards, and flowers. When I showed Gayani's card, together with all the other gifts, to my husband, he wondered if she was expressing her desire for me through the poem. Intrigued, I showed the poem to a few of my colleagues and they also thought it could well be a poem expressing lesbian desires. During the next visit I asked Gayani what she meant by this poem and she said, without any hesitation, that it expressed her love and appreciation for me. Talking about why she chose certain metaphors, she said that she loves me because I do not seem to care about class boundaries and love FTZ workers as they are. "When I return from work and I see that you are in the boarding house, it makes me happy. It is a good day when you come. Not just for me but for all of us. We love to talk to you. You listen to us and sometimes you look like you are about to cry. And some days you do cry, especially if one of us cries. And your eyes are beautiful, especially when they are filled with tears. Padmi and I sometimes gaze at you when you listen to our stories, to see the tears. And those tears are for everybody. That's what I was trying to say in the poem."

Reading the above text, one of my colleagues again said that it does seem like Gayani desires me more than as just a friend. Although some of her descriptions appear to convey that impression, when I was listening to her it was plain to see that what she was trying to explain was a deep appreciation for someone from a different social background who cared, and listened. This was a moment that made it clear for me that some of the linguistic play one encounters is untranslatable without reading the gestures and contextual nuances. However, not having readily available everyday Sinhala words to talk about homosexual desires makes it difficult for young women to understand and recognize their own desires without resorting to familiar tropes such as friendship, mentorship, and solidarity.

At the same focus group where I discussed the words for desire, I also discussed words for homosexuality. Everyone knew the term for homosexuality (*sama lingika*), but they said that they do not normally use that word in everyday conversations. The women said they might use "someone who is a little different," together with facial signs, to describe a homosexual person. Ten workers said that although they knew the word, they had never uttered it as the topic of homosexuality had never come up. Four women thought there were no lesbians in Sri Lanka; some others were not sure but thought that could be true. Two, in fact, thought homosexuality means relationships among men and said they had never heard of women having sex with women. Three said that they heard rumors of lesbian desire and relationships. No one volunteered to supply the everyday Sinhala word for lesbianism (*appa gahanawa*, literally, making hoppers), but after I provided the term, four of them said that they were aware of it. At least five others indicated that they had heard it before, while debating whether lesbianism existed in Sri Lanka. According to them, this term is considered highly stigmatizing, and although they knew it, they felt an unexplainable fear of uttering it.

Recalling Judith Butler's argument about why some forms of sexuality lack appropriate vocabulary would be useful here. According to Butler, the absence/lack of a vocabulary has to do with powerful social forces that determine how we think about desire and pleasure refusing to identify and recognize certain modes of sexuality (2009: iii) and ensuring that these "undesirable" types of sexuality are unutterable, unthinkable, and thus unlivable.

This book focuses mainly on heterosexual premarital sex. Although not as stigmatizing as homosexual desire, heterosexual premarital desire, especially among women, is not normative. There really are no neutral terms to think about or talk about heterosexual desire, thus making it difficult for women to identify with their own sexual desire. These conditions in some ways make it necessary for men to coerce them for sex – and for women to resist, at least for a while. This kind of culturally understood play in flirting, enticement, and submission gets variedly played out in various cultural contexts (Yelvington 1996; Osella and Osella 1998). The lack of neutral vocabulary to think and express desire partly explains why 45 women workers who attended three focus groups said that it is impossible to enjoy sex as an unmarried woman. The fear that men would abandon them after having sex, the anxiety about fainting on the wedding day (due to the belief that non-virgins faint on the wedding stand), and the trauma associated with being unable to prove virginity on the wedding night were identified as the main reasons for this.

Some described how fearful they felt when they were told of brides being sent back to their parents' home in white saris (instead of red homecoming saris) and wilted flowers when they were not able to prove their virginity. Four women workers said that the mere thought of how ashamed their families would feel and the impact this could have on male relatives (they might commit suicide) and younger sisters (no one would marry them) alone was enough to make them avoid premarital sex. What this means is that in addition to not having words to experience their own desires and pleasures, the shaming and punishing mechanisms in place to prevent premarital sex obscure young unmarried women workers' desires, experiences and pleasures.

I earlier noted that due to normative codes, village people control their sexual urges and that occasional expressions get explained by using culturally understood mechanisms such as trances and other supernatural influences. When young unmarried women come home crying, with a running fever, or symptoms of a panic attack following a solo trip to a waterfall or the paddy fields, people in villages tend to believe that this was because she was attacked by the deity called black prince (*kalu kumara*), and parents immediately start proceedings to get her married soon. Although the practical solution of quickly getting her married seems to suggest that the young woman had become an object of someone's desire or she herself had become desirous, it would never be identified or explained in such terms. The woman's psychic struggle gets couched within culturally acceptable idioms even as it strips her of agency.

Straddling cultural discourses of both their native villages and their new urban residences around the FTZ, women workers situationally interpreted troubling moments and scenarios within their own lives. Newly arrived young women at the FTZ who are pursued by men seeking physical pleasures may go through a period of psychic struggles that sometimes manifest as trances. For example, on a nationally televised youth talent program called *Thurunu Shakthi* (young strength), which was held at the Katunayake stadium, the FTZ worker groups were frequently featured either dancing or watching others dance. On one occasion the cameras lingered on a young woman who was engaged in a solitary dance that did not conform to baila (a popular freewheeling dance) or Western dance routines. She convulsively flayed her arms and legs while her face alternately held expressions of anguish or ecstasy. At Saman's boarding house women talked about her in embarrassed tones, and they agreed that the woman must have gone temporarily mad or was in a trance (*yakek vehila*) and the demon that had overtaken her was doing the thrashing. They complained that the factories male officers laughed at them asking whether they also do the 'aspaya gone' dance. "*Aspaya gone*" is a childish term describing children riding stationary horses. This allusion to horse riding somehow seemed strangely fitting given this woman's dance movements. Morris (1995) holds that when possessed by spirits women are permitted to take attire, gestures, and many other privileges denied them in everyday life. She further contends that within the trance women can appropriate and play with the sexual and social privileges of masculinity (584). The woman was likely a new worker expressing her intense internal conflict regarding the open space for sexual exploration and deeply internalized notions of sexual restrain and female moral conduct.

Although not as public, I witnessed another new worker in 2010, who had been at the factory for just one week and had about four young men clamoring for her affections, expressing the same internal struggles by taking off all her clothes and jumping on the bed while screaming at the top of her lungs. In another incident a worker and her family used culturally accepted reasons to explain her sudden sexual insanity. Deepthi fell hard for a man and spent a week with him in her room without coming out to go to work or the grocery store. At the end of the first week, her parents came and forcibly took her home. During the struggle to get her into the van, Deepthi hung onto a bed post and screamed obscenities at her parents giving details of her sexual escapades. Her brother dragged her by her hands and feet into the van. One year later, when I met her just before her marriage (a proposed marriage her parents had arranged), she said that her FTZ lover Nihal had given her a hypnotic medicine hidden inside an oil cake, which upon eating made her fall crazily in love with him. Her sister told me that Deepthi had not had sex knowingly and, therefore, only her body was defiled. She further noted that as the antidote that was administered had cleansed Deepthi's body, she was now as good as a virgin. Apparently, it is important to have cultural explanations that would deny or minimize an unmarried woman's agency in sexual acts. In such a context, it is not surprising that women workers' acts, explanations, and performances are fraught with ambivalences.

"Bad girls" speak freely

Although women did not directly speak of sexual desires or accept that they themselves have engaged in sexual intercourse, when something goes wrong many such self-restrictions become unusable, allowing them to speak freely of their sex lives. My close association with three activists, working among garment workers who got into trouble due to sexual activities, partly helped me obtain explicit narratives of sexual activities. I selected 12 women out of this group to conduct life history interviews in 2012, 2013, and 2014. The data from two life histories are included below. A synopsis of Sachni's life history is included to show that there are women workers who do not follow societal norms or even norms espoused by their FTZ colleagues with regard to sexual desires.

Achala

The NGO activists introduced me to Achala saying she was a good, young woman who had unfortunately made a mess of things (*okkoma wada waraddagena*). Achala had one abortion and then had a baby out of wedlock with a man whom she still remembered fondly. After describing how kind and gentle he was, she also explained why she willingly had sex with him for three years. "He used to call me *sudu* (fair one) and *baba* (baby) and when he used those words, touching my arms, and looking at my face with half closed eyes, I got all crazy (*pissu wattala gannawa*). He complimented me during sex and was very appreciative of the pleasures I gave him. He always inquired 'whether I am pleasured enough (*sathutu unada? athida?*) before getting his pleasure." According to Achala, the man could not get married because his parents had agreed to his marrying someone else from the time he was a child. She did not mind as he lived with her and swore daily that he loved her more. So even after the abortion she did not ask him to use condoms or take precautions herself. After she conceived again, Achala wanted to keep the baby, and the man went to his village promising to talk to his family about breaking up the arranged proposal. He sent her two letters but thereafter went silent. By the time Achala realized he was not coming back, it was too late to get an abortion. She approached the NGO to discuss her options and they, after some effort, convinced her to give the baby up for adoption.

Achala confessed that her particular situation prevented her from lying about sexual relations. "I mean, I was living with him in a boarding room, and I told both the boarding auntie and other girls that I was married to him. That made it so much easier to enjoy sex without always looking behind my shoulders. Sometimes girls close to me asked for advice and I told them about how he cared for my pleasure too." Showing the complexities they daily grapple with and how difficult it is to own their desires and sexual pleasures, she did say that if she had not gotten pregnant and was in a position to masquerade as a "good girl" she would likely have lied to me about enjoying sex.

Sachini

Sachini's story is somewhat atypical in that she was more directly expressive about her sexual desires than any of the other workers I talked to. She was also very young when I first met her. Several NGO staff members first told me about her as they were helping her in a court case. She had been coming to the NGO organized dancing classes for a few months and looked plump (*pirichcha*) and pretty. She came to class one Sunday, and the next thing they heard was that she had a baby on the factory shop floor the following morning. She had claimed that she did not know she was pregnant. Given that she was 17 many people took pity on her and helped her through the birth and the first few months thereafter. The NGO was helping her file the court case to get child maintenance payments, a case that she eventually won. The next year when I visited in July, the same NGO staff members were angry with her for running around with two other men. Now the father of the baby, who first denied paternity, was trying to get full custody of the baby, because, as he claimed, "The mother is using his money to have fun with men."

Two years later I managed to sit Sachini down for an interview through a boarding house owner who intermittently helped her, which then led to a close, enduring friendship. Sachini said she always liked boys and enjoyed having sex. She also liked to go places and see movies with them. She reiterated that she did not know she was pregnant at the time and said if she knew she would have definitely had an abortion. She thought she was too young to get pregnant by having sex just two times. She now knew better and used the pill as protection. She did not think her male partners have STDs and did not insist on condoms. Sachini did not have to work regularly as the maintenance money was enough to support her and the child and because her boarding house owner loved the baby and provided free child care. "I feel very confident now. All the bad things that could happen, happened to me. Now I am like a man. I choose men and if they do not make me happy, I drop them. I learn new things from magazines and try those on them. A few months ago I had two boyfriends at the same time. Now only one. I don't lie to them. I am not serious about any of these relationships. I am still young. I will start working again when the baby is in preschool." Sachini said. When I asked her about marriage, she hesitated a little and said, "One day when I am 25 or so, if someone good comes along I might get married. If my parents insisted and if someone can be good to me and my son I might agree to a proposed marriage too. But I won't marry just for the sake of getting married (*badinnan wale*). It has to be someone good with whom I can enjoy life." Then as an afterthought she added, "It has to be someone that I would want to go to bed with. Someone who is good looking, who takes daily showers and someone who can provide for us."

As noted earlier, Sachini is an atypical FTZ worker and even after interviewing some of her friends, the boarding auntie, and NGO staff who knew her, I could not pinpoint a reason why she had not internalized some of the behavioral norms as intensely as others. Interestingly, she was considered a beautiful young woman, and I was struck by how many times people commented that she could be one of my younger sisters. Unlike some of the other workers who tried middle class clothing – jeans, tight skirts, certain shirts – Sachini looked comfortable and natural in such attire even though she, like the other workers, hailed from a rural, working class family. The confidence in herself (mostly based on her good looks) seemed the reason that she appeared not to have the same concerns about reputation, marriage, and respectability.

Sexual worlds

The fact that fellow garment workers, NGO officials, the boarding owners, and even I were surprised by Sachini's story speak to how rare such attitudes and world views are among FTZ workers and young women in general. Achala's experience followed the usual trajectory among workers who got involved with deceitful men. Women who did not have such telltale signs of bad girl conduct managed their individual reputations and talked about their own sexual desires cryptically, if ever. Of course, unlike Sachini, they still had the potential of getting into a conventional marriage and policed their own expressions of sexual desire and its many actualizations. However, most workers had no problems talking about many other ways in which their sexual knowledge, perceptions, and experiences expanded since arriving at the FTZ. The following chapters analyze how FTZ workers gained sexual knowledges via pornographic magazines, dealt with sexual harassment and violence, and the reactions and responses they elicited as a result. All chapters evidence the unrecognizability and unutterability of desires leading the way to contradictory expressions and performances in boarding houses, the FTZ area, and on the streets.

Notes

1 *Kinihiriya Mal* ran for months to packed audiences and received glowing reviews in the mainstream media. However, *Niveka* and *Dabindu* (two NGO magazines), critiqued the movie for the stereotypical image it promoted. According to *Dabindu* (June 2000), *Kinihiriya Mal* ended up becoming the anvil that hammered a disadvantageous image of FTZ women even further into the public psyche.

2 Silva and Eisenberg (1996), in their study of premarital sex among Sri Lankan youth, also refer to such sexual activities, especially among Sri Lankan university students, that safeguard virginity while providing sexual gratification (6).

3 Both these scenarios were addressed, respectively, by Eshani Ruwanpura (2011) and Monica Smith (2010).

References

Butler, J. (2009) AIBR. Revista de Antropología Iberoamericana. www.aibr.org Volumen 4, Número 3: i–xiii. Madrid: Antropólogos Iberoamericanos en.

Hewamanne, S. (2003) Performing Disrespectability: New Tastes, Cultural Practices and Identity Performances by Sri Lanka's Free Trade Zone Garment Factory Workers. *Cultural Dynamics*. 15 (1). pp. 71–101.

Kondo, D. (1997) *About Face: Performing Race in Fashion and Theater*. New York: Routledge.

Morris, R.C. (1995) All Made Up: Performance Theory and the New Anthropology of Sex and Gender. *Annual Review of Anthropology*. 24. pp. 567–592.

Osella, C. and Osella, F. (1998) Friendship and Flirting: Micro-Politics in Kerala, South India. *Journal of the Royal Anthropological Institute*. 4. pp. 189–206.

Ruwanpura, E. (2011) Sex or Sensibility? The Making of Chaste Women and Promiscuous Men in a Sri Lankan University Setting (*The University of Edinburgh*, 2011–11–22).

Silva, K. Tudor and Eisenberg, Merrill. (1996) Attitude Toward Pre-marital Sex in a Sample of Sri Lankan Youth. Paper presented at the National Convention on Women's Studies, Center for Women's Research. Sri Lanka.

Smith, M. (2010) Erasure of Sexuality and Desire: State Morality and Sri Lankan Migrants in Beirut, Lebanon. *The Asia Pacific Journal of Anthropology*. 11 (3–4). pp. 378–393.

Willis, P. (1993) Symbolic Creativity. In Gray, A. and McGuigan, J. (eds.). *Studying Culture: An Introductory Reader*. London: Edward Arnold. pp. 108–120.

Yelvington, K. (1996) Flirting in the Factory. *Journal of Royal Anthropological Institution*. 31. pp. 119–165.

3 Romance on the street

Sexual banter and sexual harassment

In late August 2014, a cell phone video of a young woman slapping a man at the Wariyapola bus terminal started making the rounds on internet sites. Apparently the man had been sexually harassing the young woman for a while and the latter then reacted by repeatedly slapping him. The video's circulation led to an online comment war between the man's supporters/defenders (almost exclusively men) and those they called feminists (mostly women and a few men). The former were incensed by the woman's "unacceptable" and "unbecoming" behavior and several men goaded the humiliated man to go to a hospital and thereafter file a court case against the woman. A week later the assaulted man did just that: he complained that being slapped had led to hearing loss and filed a police report. The woman was asked to come to the police station and was then produced before a judge before being bailed out.[1] Many rights organizations supported her defense. A few days later the man was arrested on sexual harassment charges. He pleaded guilty in July 2015 and was given a six month jail term in addition to a fine of Rs. 50,000.[2] Charges against the woman were dropped, and the judge reportedly admonished the police to follow the country's laws rather than acting on baseless rumors and public opinion.[3]

The laws the judge was referring to pertain to sexual harassment. According to the Penal Code (Amendment) Act, No. 22 of 1995 (section 345), sexual harassment is an offense, described as: "Harassment of a sexual nature using assault, criminal force, or words or actions which causes annoyance to the person being harassed." The punishment for the offence is imprisonment with or without hard labor for any period up to five years; or a fine; or imprisonment and a fine.[4] Many legal and human rights activists and women's organizations hailed the final outcome of this incident and predicted that more women would now come forward and complain about sexual harassment. This incident in the national and social media played itself out even as FTZ factory workers in Katunayake situationally defined, used, and ignored legal and middle class narratives on sexual harassment. The other parties that concerned themselves with FTZ workers, such as NGO officials, police, and government officials, also shaped these responses in different ways.

This chapter analyzes how the laws and discourses surrounding sexual harassment play out at the ground level. By focusing on sexual banter between female

FTZ workers and working class males in the FTZ area – including workers' boarding house cluster areas, main bus terminal, bazaars, and the streets surrounding the FTZ – the chapter demonstrates how sexual meanings are contextually negotiated. By examining women workers' varied engagement in sexual banter on city streets, I make two major arguments. First, the meanings associated with sexual vocabulary and acts are contextually negotiated and participating in sexual banter can empower women by allowing them identities outside the dominant mores of respectability. Second, by uncritically adopting Western notions of sexual harassment to condemn sexual banter between working class men and women on city streets, NGOs, and varied government agencies have inadvertently colluded in the capitalist global scheme to produce docile working class women who follow rules of respectability and thereby ensure an ideal assembly line workforce. The workers' reluctance to be disciplined in the way that these elites expected make them, yet again, transgressive women who do not abide by global narratives on what is sexual harassment.

Sanitizing the streets

"Sri Lanka is the only country in South Asia that has a criminal law specifically recognizing sexual harassment as a crime," proudly proclaimed a report published by the Friedric Ebert Foundation of Sri Lanka.[5] According to a leading human rights lawyer on the island, "The sexual harassment law applies to the work place, buses and education institutions and the private as well as public sector."[6] This broad applicability stems from the wording dealing with power relations in the amendment to the penal code, which specifically refers to: "Unwelcome sexual advances by words or action used by a person in authority (such as police, armed service personnel, school officials, medical officials etc.)."[7]

Interestingly, FTZ NGO activists often complain that the problem in Sri Lanka is not the lack of laws but women's reluctance to come forward and complain about unwelcome sexual conduct. As a project officer at the NGO, Diri Piyasa, noted, "The laws are mostly about the work place. But in the FTZ area sexual harassment is happening everyday on the streets. Groups of men follow women workers and make fun of them, tell sexist jokes . . . and these women, they just laugh and blush. We need to educate these young women about how such acts constitute an affront to all women. Almost all our workshops have a component on sexual harassment and how to deal with it and how to make use of the new laws to punish the offenders."[8] Obviously, a lot of attention is paid to sexual harassment in and around the FTZ, with contesting ideas and approaches on how to deal with it.

During the past few years, I have interacted closely with four NGOs that work tirelessly to improve conditions for female workers. They are concerned about sexual harassment on city streets and target speeches and activities to educate female workers on why they must be offended when certain acts occur and complain to the proper authorities. NGO workshop attendees were vocal about incidents of public harassment and actively participated in formulating action plans to stop such behavior by men. However, when I was with them, most workers appeared to take pleasure in participating in some of the very activities that they condemned at the workshops. Confusion, perhaps, is understandable since the activities that NGO workers and police label "uncivilized" and "cruel" to women are much more complex and fluid in their varied manifestations and can be difficult to summarily categorize as harassing behavior. Working class men and women both seek to communicate through group banter while walking to and from work, especially on Sundays when they visit the bazaar. Many female FTZ workers who attend NGO workshops on sexual harassment also derive immense satisfaction from engaging in group sexual banter on city streets. Thus, they complicate attempts to "sanitize" the supposedly "unruly" city streets and marketplaces.

I have analyzed elsewhere how workers daily contest both the spatial and metaphorical boundaries to constrain and structure their lives that institutional and private forces set and reshape (Hewamanne 2008a). The new gendered and classed subjects of the Katunayake FTZ were produced within the social, cultural space of the city precisely through this struggle, and their responses to NGOs, police, and neighbors' maneuverings are significant aspects of this struggle. Women rejected middle class attempts to label public performances of sexual banter as sexual harassment even as they conveniently appropriated the very same middle class rhetoric to deal with disagreeable moments within the same group performances. Women workers' delight in participating in these exchanges registers their refusal to be governed by technologies of self that get disseminated by the media and NGO workshops as appropriate for "modern, educated, and urban women." Thus women's performances in public spaces convey a specific classed and gendered interpretation of sexual discourses. It not only marks their difference from middle class men and women but also represents one of the many ways they participate in subaltern politics of citizenship.

Class sexualities, imported norms, and regulatory forces

Many studies have focused on sexual harassment in the workplace, especially with regard to restaurant and female factory workers (Giuffre and Williams 1994; Yelvington 1996; Gruber 1998; Williams et al. 1999; Bender 2004; Lerum 2004; Jensen 2005; Barraclough 2006). Many among them have noted that sexualized banter in the workplace serves as a mechanism of control and reproduces existing gender hierarchies: men initiate sexualized speech play, and women tolerate it passively (MacKinnon 1979; Uggen and Blackstone 2004). Bender notes that at the turn of the twentieth century, male workers in garment sweatshops used sexual harassment to construct and reproduce definitions of skill and justify unequal pay (2004). Based on ethnographic research on contemporary assembly line work in transnational factories, both Yelvington (1996) and Salzinger (2000, 2003) describe sexualized speech, acts, and physical contact as ways through which men seek to control women. They characterize women's participation in such exchanges as conforming and accommodating to existing gender hierarchies.

However, a number of scholars have engaged in more multifaceted analyzes addressing questions of representation and intersections of race, gender, and social class. According to Jensen (2005), nineteenth-century European working class men and women engaged in pleasurable erotic conduct that resulted in the entire working class being labeled "bawdy bodies" (2005). Barraclough (2006) analyzed middle class writings on sexual harassment in early twentieth-century Korean factories and maintains that they represent factory workers as sexual victims of industrialization and thus deny them political voice. Some studies, especially focusing on the restaurant industry, indicate that both men and women may benefit from workplace sexual banter as it leads to camaraderie among co-workers (Williams et al. 1999; Lerum 2004).

Osella and Osella (1998) discuss sexual joking, teasing, and flirting among young people in Kerala, South India. They claim that rather than reproducing rigid gender hierarchies, sexual banter indicates ambiguity, indeterminacy, and ambivalence in everyday social life. They note that to see sexual banter as reinforcing existing gender hierarchies is to "underestimate the extent to which gender and hierarchy can be played as a game" (195). The following analysis extends this argument. It dissects the aesthetic nuances of sexualized banter to show that this is one place where women perform their desires.

By focusing on NGO workshops and other educational activities that seek to curb sexual harassment against garment workers, I shed light on the new disciplinary regimes created around working class men and women's lives. While noting the importance of rules and regulations governing workplace behavior, this chapter highlights how NGOs fail to consider cultural and class differences and struggles over the meaning of "appropriate sexual mores." This failure becomes even more evident when considering that the NGOs' unlikely partners in educating workers on modern sexual harassment attitudes are workers' neighbors.

Many neighbors see sexual banter on the streets as shameful womanly behavior and a marker of how FTZ work and migration corrupt young women and seek to discipline them whenever they can. Therefore, by uncritically adopting Western notions of sexual harassment to condemn all sexual banter on city streets, NGOs unintentionally collude with middle class forces that look down on FTZ garment workers as unruly and corrupt. This chapter therefore will problematize the harassment discourses pertaining to female FTZ workers by analyzing some incidents that highlight the interplay between dominant and alternative class and gender expectations and individual agency.

Not even looks and glances should be tolerated

This is fairly standard advice provided by NGOs. The NGOs to which I was closest had different origins and organizational hierarchies. Diri Piyasa was an arm of the Ministry of Women's Affairs and therefore closely mimicked the mainstream state line. Both Mithurusevene and Janasetha were local branches of Colombo-based national NGOs, which operated with financial support from well-known international NGOs, and both were supposed to execute plans formulated by

Colombo offices. Staff members were critical of the iron-fisted approach of some Colombo officials, and some expressed frustration over their unrealistic demands. By 2015, both these latter organizations were defunct – although the staff found positions within other NGOs and labor alliances, allowing me to continue collaborating with them.

Dabindu was an autonomous, grassroots organization that now depends on foreign funds. While staff members of the other three organizations belong to middle class families, Dabindu activists have working class backgrounds and a history of association with trade unions. Unfortunately, their attitude toward sexual banter on city streets did not differ much from the position held by the other organizations: they all held that sexualized speech is bad and should be eliminated by educating women against participating in it.[9] Their understanding of sexual harassment, women's empowerment, and liberation seems influenced by, first, their upbringing in a society where the image of the ideal woman is promoted through school curricula and media and, second, their participation in global donor circuits that prioritize certain programs, such as education against sexual harassment.

According to several NGO officials, their activism was instrumental in the Ceylon Chamber of Commerce and the Employers Federation of Ceylon launching a code of conduct against sexual harassment at work in December 2007. In March 2006, NGOs organized a mass rally of FTZ workers to protest sexual harassment on the roads and in other public spaces around the FTZ. NGO staff from both Dabindu and Mithurusevene were vocal at this rally. Chamila Thushari of Dabindu described the situation: "Men fondle girls walking on the roads or standing by the side of the roads, at the bazaar or the bus stands, and make insulting comments. It is so bad that it discourages women from going to work."[10] Later, Jayanthi, a SAFE (Safe and Free Employees) convener and staff member told me that "The NGO charter on sexual harassment notes that even looks or loving glances (*alma, balma*) are not allowed if they are unsolicited. I think that here (in the Katunayake area), the problem is not work place harassment but the groups of men who follow women and make sexist comments. Women just have to ignore or smile back. That's why we are trying to give them the necessary tools to respond to this bad behavior."[11] This understanding that unsolicited acts constitute sexual harassment is at odds with FTZ workers' nuanced, contextual negotiation of such (anticipated) acts within FTZ public spaces.

Sexual harassment or romantic communication?

During my varied fieldwork stints, I observed and experienced various activities and noticed that women had different definitions and nuanced understandings of what an average outsider might term *sexual harassment*. I explore their contextual interpretations through several vignettes, beginning in April 2000.

"There! There! That army *aiya* [elder brother] is looking at us. Look! He will say something now," said Kanchana as she pushed me to the left so I could take a good look at the lone Air Force sentry standing by the green barrels around the checkpoint. The entire group of women tensed in happy anticipation, and some erupted into uncontrollable giggles as we neared it.

Two more Air Force soldiers, grinning widely, emerged from behind the bunker-like structure. "Ah, *nangi* [younger sister], seems like you are off shopping," a soldier called from his place beside the barrels.

"Tell them to go and protect Jaffna [where the civil war was raging at the time] instead of dozing around in Colombo," said Kalyani, pretending to talk to Kanchana but saying it loud enough for the soldiers to hear.

"*Ane*, is there a better job than protecting these sisters?" the next soldier chimed in, just as our group passed the checkpoint.

Turning toward the soldiers Nadee said, "No wonder we are losing the war." We heard their laughter for another few minutes while we giggled our way toward the Averiwatthe junction.

"Today, they did not have time to pass out their addresses. Some days, they push address notes into our hands so quickly, you don't even know who gave you what," Kalyani explained to me, turning back to wave at the three soldiers, who looked on smiling.

NGO activists usually refer to such incidents as sexual harassment. During my initial research in the FTZ area in 1997 and 1998 and in the early part of my 1999–2000 research, I too associated such incidents with sexual harassment and considered them among the most difficult experiences for workers and researchers. However, since my long research stint in 2000, when I lived closely with the workers, and visits almost every year from 2002 to 2015, I realized that some of these activities operate on a different register.

The workers in the above incident never directly solicited or gave consent to the soldiers' attentions and remarks, but body language and banter amply evidenced that they were not averse to the attention and in fact seemed very happy to be talked to. Thus, FTZ workers' perception of harassment differed somewhat from the middle class perception, which is borrowed from Western discourses. Women workers do not agree that all catcalls represent harassment. Many women I interviewed said they enjoyed the catcalls since they showed the men's interest in them. Catcalls have initiated many a romantic relationship, they informed me. "I would prefer a boy to approach me directly or perhaps send a letter, but boys are shy, too. If a girl says no to a boy, other boys make fun of him, so it is good first to make sure that the girl likes him before approaching directly," Janaki explained. This finding is similar to Osella and Osella's (1998) observation about flirting in Kerala, South India. According to them, just as in popular films, men initiate romances through sexual banter.

Many men who frequented the area congregated in groups and initiated advances toward women as part of a group activity.[12] Usually, catcalls were limited to funny remarks and jokes. Women showed their interest or lack thereof through body language, and the men proceeded accordingly. When women were in a group, this process became easier since a particular woman's friends would start communicating with the male group. While the two groups stood or walked at a respectable distance, they exchanged jovial remarks that more or less informed each other about the individual man and woman's intentions and, if necessary, where to meet again. Even when no long-term interests were expressed, groups of women enjoyed and encouraged catcalls and even sexist jokes. Some women shouted back in a jovial manner, and others just laughed, making eye-contact with the men.[13]

Many group encounters led to much more direct sexual banter. For example, in 2004 I was with a group of FTZ workers in the bazaar when a group of young men started walking behind us, making comments about how beautiful we looked that day. Their comments soon focused on the *nangi* [younger sister] in the pink dress who seemed to have stolen the heart of a *malli* [younger brother] in their group. While both *nangi* and *malli* were blushing furiously and admonishing the others to be quiet, the friends of the two enthusiastically continued. When Sita noted that the *nangi* in the pink dress (a common style of speech in these encounters) would never marry and intended to live a religious life, a young man said, "Oh, what a waste! Cobwebs will gather in that place [*athana makunu del bendei*]." The men roared with laughter, and the women blushed, but Sita countered, "How do we know that you are not corroded?" Several young men assured us that there was no danger of corrosion. That was when usually shy Vijitha said, "Then these people must be like Prince *Hasthamalaka*" [Hasthamalaka literally means *flower in the hand*]. This time, the men blushed. They recovered quickly and, roaring with laughter, noted how corrupt these *nangies* were. I especially remember one young man striking an exaggerated pose considered stereotypically transgendered in Sri Lanka. With hands on hips, he said in a high-pitched voice, "*aaane*, these *nangies* are naughty, naughty, naughty" [aa*ane me nangila naughty, naughty, naughty*]. Another young man quickly took a serious tone, saying, "So what are we going to do about this poor boy's burning heart?" Then he switched to a joking tone, "Do you want to see his body hanging from that tree tomorrow morning?" Another man joined in: "I will hold that *nangi* in the blue shirt [referring to the most vocal, Sita] personally responsible for the tragedy." After about 10–15 more minutes of funny exchanges, Sita said, "We are not promising anything, but she takes the FDK bus from the eighteenth mile post at 7.00 in the morning", at which point, Shirani, the *nangi* in pink, made a big fuss, slapping Sita's hand and reprimanding her for providing too much information. A week later, Shirani and the boy with the burning heart, Nimal, had become a couple and were still dating at the time my fieldwork ended.

As noted in Chapter 1, by 2015 cell phones and texting were common place among FTZ workers and the young men who vied for their attention. Yet, this kind of intimate, humorous group banter still occurred and was excitedly anticipated. For instance, in August 2015, a group of boys started following the women I was with and expressed one young man's interest in a woman who was already engaged to another man. The woman herself showed her unwillingness to the proposal through facial gestures and miming slapping motions. The boys in response indicated that the suitor is in the military by mimicking shooting actions and sounds. This communication, for no apparent reason, occurred across the road as the two groups stood at bus stops at opposite sides. The women quickly decided that the men were lying about the military connection (judging by the clothes and demeanor) and decided to show that the woman concerned was involved with a more powerful military man by mimicking a bomb explosion. Although I thought it was poor miming, the message was well received given that the men responded by mimicking in ways that suggested they were being hit or choked. As we moved on, we heard them calling for other women to make the man happy, and laughingly comforted him by jokingly saying women have black hearts and are universally untrustworthy. This exchange was excitedly shared among the other workers at the boarding house and I was later told that the woman later relished narrating the incident to her boyfriend.

Apart from these incidents, when women walked in groups, men who traveled in buses, trucks, or on bicycles slowed down to shout a compliment or make a joke. While this annoyed me in the beginning, I soon noted that my companions giggled or shouted back and, after returning to the boarding houses, related these stories with enthusiasm. They were, for the most part, taken as a sign of appreciation. Police officers stationed in the area, just like the military men at checkpoints, did not hesitate to make remarks when groups of women walked past them. When the women were in groups they always responded to such remarks with smiles or retorts and were regarded with happiness and pride. When I discussed this situation with Dabindu activist Chamila Thushari, she said that once when she confronted a policeman who made a pass at a group of women, he replied saying "If we do not say anything, they would hit us with a banana skin or something to provoke us."

Although they enjoyed and looked forward to catcalls, jokes, and sexual innuendos, all the women I talked to thoroughly detested men who darted up in crowded places to whisper obscene words in their ears. The women felt doubly harassed since they could not respond in kind. They also said they disliked any uninvited touching. It soon became apparent that there was a locally understood, somewhat fuzzy line between what was encouraged and opposed. For example, during group exchanges in crowded places, such as the Sunday fair, temple festivals, and on trips home, women typically enjoyed being touched or squeezed by men and reciprocated in kind. I witnessed women initiating such touching at a temple festival once and heard that it happened occasionally. However, if a man touched or fondled them while speeding by on a motor bike, women usually got angry as that only represented lewd intentions as opposed to the negotiated touching that resulted from group banter.

Their approval or disapproval of such behavior seemed based on the nature of the persons catcalling, especially the age group, and the possibilities for further association. FTZ workers wanted to have boyfriends and experienced a great deal of peer pressure to have boyfriends. Since their factories employed only a few male workers, they could only meet men through their leisure activities in the area. Therefore, unlike middle class women, they considered catcalls and some other acts generally termed sexual harassment as fulfilling a necessary social function. Catcalls allowed young people in a non-permissive society to express their initial interest in each other and to enjoy cross-sexual communication. Workers did not welcome every comment or all physical advances. They contextually decided what actions demanded a favorable response and what should be termed reprehensible. Women considered older men who catcalled or tried to touch them perverts or mentally challenged. Such men did not have peer groups, were easily found out, and most faced swift street justice. That might be the reason why such acts are rare (as per my interviews with police officers, neighbors, and workers).

While the man's intentions, age and opportunity for further relations constitute major criteria in deciding whether catcalls are welcomed, a woman's character traits, such as how skillfully she can make a wisecrack or how invested she is in projecting an image similar to ideal expectations, also figure into the decision-making process. In creating this space for cross-sexual communication, these women combine different cultural knowledges to respond to the new demands of their lives as factory workers. Such communication relies on the safety of gendered groups and is probably influenced by village experiences where most verbal exchanges occur across gendered groups. However, the FTZ workers use such communication as a stepping stone for male-female relationships and accept and enjoy the physical contact that occurs within this context. They have recreated the culturally accepted communicative space to express, mostly through performances, the emotional and physical desires that flourish under conducive FTZ area conditions.

I am not suggesting that village youth do not use group communication to advance romantic relationships. In fact, several women told me they had witnessed such incidents in village temples and near open-air bathing facilities. Within the closely controlled social spaces of villages, however, such exchanges can never be as sexualized as the FTZ exchanges. Writing about joking circles among urban youth in India, Kirin Narayan (1993: 178) notes that the changing content of urban jokes is a good indication of transformations in social norms and economic values. Similarly, the sexualized character of FTZ workers' banter reflects emerging working class sexual mores in urban spaces.

Being familiar with less intense forms of group exchange in their villages deterred many FTZ workers from acting on the new knowledges they acquired through NGO educational activities and media exposure. In fact, they rejected the NGOs' wholesale appropriation of Western vocabulary on workplace sexual harassment and chose to determine it contextually. Often, they eagerly awaited these cross-gender communications initiated as catcalls. What a middle class feminist considers an instance of sexual harassment represents part of their journey toward empowerment: most of them, especially until cell phones became common place around 2010 or so, found their boyfriends by participating in this communicative space. Although now the "missed call method" – calling random numbers and thereby initiating conversations – has become popular among workers, the more social character of group banter is still frequently employed for cross-sexual communication.

NGO workshops: teaching how to be modern

All NGOs working in or near the FTZ conducted educational programs and distributed pamphlets and other educational materials among workers, focusing on such topics as reproductive health, sexual harassment, and HIV-AIDS prevention.

Explicit basic facts were delivered with the overall message that to learn certain behavior patterns (knowledge of contraceptives) and social responses (say no to sexual jokes) is to be *modern*. Although workers faced sexualized commentary on the streets, the NGO workshops normally used Western literature on workplace harassment.

For example, during a NGO workshop for FTZ workers, a speaker distributed pamphlets with drawings intended to show them how to recognize an instance of sexual harassment. One depicted a woman seated before an office typewriter, while a man stood with his hip against her shoulder saying, "So sorry! It happened by mistake." This pamphlet was very much on target for female employees working in mixed sex environments who often complained of such experiences. FTZ workers, however, work in mostly female environments, and their immediate supervisors are usually female. They have only limited interactions with male managers, who usually take pains to keep the class distance between them alive.

This disconnection with their immediate surroundings was made clear when I realized that workers often use the "it is a mistake" tactic for fun. When groups of men bumped into women at nightly musical shows, at the fair, or in tour buses during pleasure trips they usually uttered something similar to "sorry, it is a mistake", and both men and women typically ended up laughing and exchanging more information. During one pleasure trip, men and women who were dancing in the aisles of the hired bus bumped into each other every time the driver applied the brakes, which was often. Egging on the driver to brake harder, groups bumped into each other, while both men and women gleefully yelled, "*Sorry meya, veradila happune*" [sorry dear, I bumped onto you by mistake]. However, by 2015, this practice seems to have died out, perhaps because cell phones now made it possible to conduct some of the same performances using the "missed call" tactic.

Stop: sexual harassment is a crime!

Many say that in Sri Lanka, especially in the FTZ, women cannot perpetrate sexual harassment. However, I once witnessed one-sided bullying of a lone young man by FTZ workers. About ten residents of Saman's boarding house, including myself, embarked on a day trip to visit Varana temple. We had decided to use public transportation, the most common mode of travel for FTZ workers, but when I saw how crowded the buses were, I said that I would be happy to contribute enough to hire a private vehicle. Overhearing that our hired van was heading directly to the Varana temple, a well-dressed young man asked the driver if he could join us, as he was traveling to a place near the temple. After he agreed to pay a sum that was slightly more than the normal bus fare, he was allowed to get in, and he sat in the single seat by the door. He looked as if he worked in a Colombo office, and his demeanor definitely differed from that of most other men who frequent the FTZ.

The workers started with mild teasing, but his unresponsiveness frustrated them, and the teasing escalated into jokes filled with sexual innuendos. He was not prepared for these sexually charged jokes and furiously blushed and looked down at his shoes throughout the two-hour journey. When he got out just before the temple, the women laughingly shouted at him through the windows asking him to be "more manly."

It was interesting to note how their verbal response was colored by existing models of gender, even as they were inverting it. I also found it fascinating that the young man was put through this ordeal right under a poster on sexual harassment sponsored by the Ministry of Women's Affairs that adorned the side of the bus. Ironically, it depicted a lusty-looking man pushing against a tearful young woman, while the text screamed, "Stop! Sexual harassment is a crime."

That female workers welcomed and sometimes initiated such physical contact does not mean that NGOs have no reason to be concerned. As noted earlier, the workers universally detested men who whispered obscene words or men who stood at dark corners and displayed their genitals. On several occasions, nightly musical shows became nightmares for workers, as progressively more drunken men lost sense of the fine balance between welcome and unwelcome behavior. In 2000, many workers said they would not go to these shows or only go in large groups or with male friends to avoid such incidents. By 2006, the situation appeared to have improved, as police officers showed a strong interest in curtailing behavior that had made these entertainment activities unsafe for female workers. By 2015, many workers noted that they have no qualms about going to musical shows at night.

Since 1995, several NGOs and the Ministry of Women's Affairs have been conducting sexual harassment awareness workshops for police officers, and they seem to have had a positive impact in the Katunayake area. In January 2008, Jayanthi, the then project coordinator at Janasetha, spoke very appreciatively of the new Officer in Charge of the Katunayake Police Station, Inspector De Pinto. She referred to an incident when he slapped two men making catcalls at FTZ workers and then threw them both into a police jeep. "He wanted to teach a lesson to everyone that the police would not take sexual harassment lightly," said Jayanthi. This new attitude could adversely affect the kind of public exchanges I described above. However, I noticed that the constables on the streets, who are also from marginalized rural communities, displayed a more nuanced understanding of the aesthetics of such sexual verbal games, knowing when a woman was willingly playing along and when she was not. They themselves participated in such exchanges from time to time and, therefore, I suspect, might not be too inclined to emulate their officers in charge.

During 2006–2009, due to increased hostilities between the LTTE (Liberation Tamil Tigers of Eelam) and government armed forces, the Katunayake International Airport area, which includes the FTZ and vicinity, had been declared a high-security zone. There was increased surveillance of groups and night-time entertainment was curtailed. The nightly musical shows had to wrap up by 10:00 p.m., and police and military personnel were diligent in breaking up any gathering on the airport road or at the main bus terminal. After the end of the war in May 2009, such security measures were reduced. This seems to have led to more nightly activities in the area and may have contributed to the present workers saying they, unlike their predecessors a decade earlier, were confident and comfortable attending such activities.

Just as in 2000 and 2008, in 2015 too workers claimed that being followed by a group of joking young men when they visited musical shows prevented drunkards from harassing them. On the few occasions I went with workers to such night shows, the women had either pre-arranged with a group of men to accompany them or aligned themselves with a male group through jokes as soon as they reached the area. The contradictory potential of sexual banter is implicit in this move: while empowering in some ways, it also reproduces some gender norms. Especially at the musical shows, banter is initiated and sustained not only because it is pleasurable but because it provides a sense of belonging and protection. In these and other situations, the men usually initiate group communication, and while the women eagerly anticipated it, their responses always included some show of reluctance conveyed through contradictory body language. At the outset at least, the exchanges are configured around the existing gender norms of men's sexual agency and women's performance of reluctance and eventual acquiescence.

The space for ambiguity created by the show of reluctance may have prompted NGO staff and the police to talk about female workers as victims of sexual harassment on city streets. However, at least one boarding house owner explicitly used NGO sexual harassment vocabulary to condemn "the couples who are glued together [*alawila*] in dark alleys" and said she had called the police several times to come and put both men and women in jail for five years, which is the maximum punishment for sexual harassment. This extreme reaction to sex, not harassment, shows why it is important to use clear wording in sexual harassment discourses. While ambiguity and varied manifestations of sexual banter underline the need for a contextual and case-specific understanding, clear wording is vital to prevent the moral police using it to crush budding female desires and sexualities.

It seems clear that neighbors and public officials, such as police officers, often take NGO viewpoints concerning sexual harassment as an affirmation of dominant sexual mores and use NGO and legal vocabulary to condemn both men and women for engaging in sexual banter and consensual sex. For example, when praising the police for being vigilant and using thin bamboo canes (*wevala*) to hit and disperse boisterous male and female groups, a group of female boarding house owners used the Sinhala words for *sexual harassment, sexual assault,* and *shameless, immoral men and women* interchangeably to talk about sexual banter. Rather than helping workers achieve their potential in the workplace, these discourses, therefore, add to the stigma attached to FTZ garment workers and in some ways have become part of the hegemonic process that seeks to achieve working class consent to dominant cultural categories. Not only were workers compelled to perform a certain persona for NGO activists and, to a lesser extent, neighbors as "women who hated sexual banter," but in some instances they had to provide excuses for having engaged in it. Ironically, most workers have figured out how to engage in and negotiate both NGO vocabulary and public sexual banter in ways benefitting them.

NGO vocabulary in daily life

Some of the encounters described above seem to suggest that NGO educational efforts had no impact on FTZ workers' understanding of incidents, exchanges, and relationships of a sexual nature. However, if asked about sexual harassment, the workers, especially those who frequented NGO offices, made clear that they were quite capable of deftly wielding the vocabulary of NGO workshops, pamphlets, posters, and other educational material. *Lingika hinsanaya* [sexual harassment] and *kanthawanta erehi prachandathwaya* [violence against women] were two topics that some FTZ workers talked about easily and passionately. Some tended to use this vocabulary whenever a researcher asked them a question that included words such as sexual harassment, oppression, and empowerment. The following vignette demonstrates how women could use Western discourses on sexual harassment to understand and respond to unsatisfactory situations that arose during desired, pleasurable banter.

Although public group exchanges were almost always initiated by male groups, opportunities to participate, respond, and tease were more or less equal as the banter went on. However, as women are encouraged to internalize notions of shame-fear more deeply than men, they became disturbed when an exchange crossed the delicate boundary that separated the acceptable from the unacceptable. One evening Madhuri stomped into the boarding room where I sat, threw herself on a bed, and started crying. Three other workers who had accompanied her on a shopping trip to Averiwatthe junction followed her into the room and told us what happened while trying to appear angry even as they giggled intermittently. They said a group of boys had started following them and commented on how beautiful Madhuri looked that day. She acted offended and started to walk away while swaying her hips in a deliberate fashion. Reacting to the rhythmical sway of her hips, one young man had commented that an excrement-producing backside had no business dancing [*rena pukata mona nalawilida*]. This remark made Madhuri tearful and caused the women to abandon the shopping trip and come back.

Hearing about it, an incensed Kalyani[14] started berating all men in the area, claiming they were ignorant and uncivilized and had no idea of women's right to live without fear of sexual harassment. "They are such morons that they don't even know that if we complained they could be put in jail for five years. Why didn't you go to the police? If we do not start complaining and getting these men to pay for their bad behavior, sexual harassment will never stop," she continued. Several others joined her, complaining that the FTZ held all the uncouth men in the country, and that women were partly to blame for condoning their terrible activities without complaining to the authorities.

By this time, Madhuri was laughing into her pillow. Seeing this, another woman who had seen what had taken place said, "I cannot really blame them. This woman really put on a show with her swaying hips." Furiously blushing and trying to hide her face in the pillow, Madhuri agreed: "It just happened when they said I looked beautiful . . ." While discussing her seemingly reflexive physical reaction, which several others said had happened to them as well, the women agreed that the man could have chosen a more delicate way to say what he did, such as singing the popular song, "*Sukomala bandha lelewa* . . ." [swaying your dainty hips]. Kalyani also abandoned the sexual harassment rhetoric and expressed happiness that the other men in the group berated the offender and made him apologize repeatedly to the women.

The shifts in Madhuri and Kalyani's reactions showed that public banter is not an easily parsed category. The ambivalence in their responses in some ways reflected their ambiguous position as rural women temporarily working in urban, transnational factories. It also reflected the difficulties they had in recognizing their own physical desires and responses, and their propensity to choose socially acceptable ways of reacting to sexually charged exchanges. They seemed unsure in choosing what was meaningful to them over what they thought the appropriate response should be. Note that Madhuri was not at all ambivalent about which room to dash into and complain about her painful experience. Neither she nor her friends stayed in that room, but she seemed to know that in my presence – the most tangible connection to some of the global discourses they were exposed to through NGOs – she would receive the most moral support, from me as well as her FTZ friends.

Regulatory forces and resistance

NGO street drama groups also addressed sexual harassment on Katunayake streets. In July 2006 I was present at a Janasetha performance on sexual harassment and sex trafficking in the FTZ area. It took place at the cramped intersection of many alleys dotted with boarding houses and attracted FTZ workers and a fair number of young men who clearly enjoyed the social messages creatively presented using entertaining street theater. Throughout the performance, I was quite intrigued to see how men and women engaged in group sexual banter and even physical contact, while the performance stressed how women were victims of sexual harassment and violence.

Both Dabindu and Janasetha maintained theater groups, mostly composed of FTZ workers, and regularly performed on the crowded streets near the bazaar on Sundays. Both women and men gathered in a circle that took up more than half the street space, and the police turned a blind eye to the obvious violation of rules, demonstrating how unique FTZ Sundays are. However, this appropriation of the streets provided only an ambiguous and contested space for social participation. While tolerated, the ways they used the space for assertive behavior and flirtation reinforced fears that the FTZ as a whole was contributing to moral degeneration and undermining the nation's purity. In one of Janasetha's street performances, a melee ensued between neighbors, NGO staff, and FTZ worker-actors. I was not present at this performance but heard accounts from several parties involved. According to NGO staff, the villagers became incensed and attacked the audience and performers, claiming that the drama on HIV-AIDS awareness suggested people in the area were engaging in casual sex and thereby gave their neighborhood a bad image.

However, a staff member of another NGO, several audience members, and some boarding house owners told me a slightly different story (at least in terms of the sequence of events that led to the skirmish). According to them, a young man and woman in the audience were getting too intimate, and an incensed elderly man from the neighborhood hit them with an empty king coconut shell, injuring the young woman sufficiently to require rushing her to the hospital. Hearing about it, some of the men associated with the NGO got angry, and an argument with the neighbors ensued, leading to physical violence. According to these informants, the neighbors beat the NGO drama troupe until they ran away. Even Jayanthi, the project coordinator, had to flee the scene and was only saved from a beating because the "big boss" of the NGO managed to get her inside their van in time.[15]

I noted earlier how Katunayake neighbors took extensive measures to dissociate themselves from the newcomers who had made their town a city. In addition to these class-based exclusionary strategies, they also acted as regulators to keep the workers from getting too unruly. In fact, the few times I witnessed street theater performances, I noticed two circles of spectators. The troupe performed in the center; the workers, both women and men, gathered loosely around; and a few paces behind, the older residents of Katunayake gathered in small groups and kept a watchful eye on the performances of both actors and young spectators. While the NGO street drama tried to educate and train workers to conduct themselves as modern urban subjects, the neighbors deployed their own surveillance and punished workers who strayed too far from the ideal image of the good Sinhala Buddhist woman. These spaces enacted the struggles of modernity, nation, gender, and sexuality over the figure of the FTZ worker, with two competing regulatory forces trying to discipline the new city and its defining inhabitants.

I have elsewhere analyzed the moral panic generated by rural women's migration to urban FTZs for work (Hewamanne 2008). While appreciated for economic development, FTZs were also considered places that corrupted innocent village women. Neighbors allowed a certain "unruliness" as long as they and their daughters were exempt from the stigma associated with FTZ workers. NGO staff also used exclusionary strategies to demarcate class boundaries. For example, some confessed to wearing saris and sunglasses to mark their difference from the workers. As one witness recounted, when the drama troupe and the NGO staff were attacked, Jayanthi had to run for safety with her saree raised to her knees. It appears that when the city's moral reputation is threatened and "remedial actions" were taken against the "wrong-doers" the symbols of social class and modernity unravel to bare the woman underneath.

Victims, agents, and social class

In the contested city spaces where dramas of nation, modernity, gender, and sexuality are performed, female FTZ workers' engagement with sexual banter finds meaning. It is also important to note that this public expressive practice is more class-based than gendered.

The educational strategies of FTZ NGOs in Sri Lanka have uncritically adopted Western feminist and legal discourses on workplace sexual harassment and overlook the fact that this kind of public group communication has been a part of youth cultures of all social classes in the past. Several Catholic school memoirs by older men relate how boys gathered in groups at bus stops to communicate with a girl one of them fancied (DeVotta 2005). Such girls seem to have been much more restrained than FTZ workers. FTZ street expressive practices have become an outdated mode of communication among cellphone-using, text-messaging Colombo youth.

Middle class Colombo youth now meet at school dances, night clubs, casinos, and mass tuition classes. For FTZ workers, whose workplaces had only few men of equal class positioning, city streets presented important sites for intimate exchanges. Distanced from the bonds of kinship, class, caste, and rank that constrained them in their villages, both men and women seem to explore their intimate desires more boldly in and around the Katunayake FTZ.

NGO enthusiasm in training FTZ workers to properly respond to incidents of sexual harassment becomes more suspicious in light of new research on the rampant sexual harassment that female executives of FTZ factories face daily at work. It reveals a masculine world in which male executives engage in explicitly sexually harassing behavior that female executives feel utterly powerless to stop. At an underwear factory, inquiries about bra sizes, going behind a somewhat large woman with a thong and commenting that it would not fit, and bringing condom-shaped balloons to a company party are some examples of behavior aimed to make female executives uncomfortable. Their feeling of powerlessness leads them to look for ways to move out while hanging onto their current jobs, which offer high pay and other benefits. Demonstrating the class complexities of sexual harassment, the male executives stated that they would not even dream of making such jokes in the presence of their subordinates, the factory workers.[16]

When I recounted these details in 2008 and 2015 among male company executives, they echoed the same sentiments, demonstrating that most felt that such actions or words could only be considered sexual harassment if directed at subordinates. Like the executives interviewed in the previous study, these officers maintained that they did not need any education on sexual harassment because they already knew how to behave with factory workers. They also viewed the underwear factory incidents as innocent fun among colleagues of equal standing and said the female executives enjoyed such "teasing." They talked about garment factory workers as victims of sexual harassment on their way to and from work from uncouth men – meaning working class men – and expressed passionate support for any measures to stop it.

However, compared to the FTZ workers, the female executives seem to need more support in dealing with sexual harassment – most urgently in the form of educational workshops for their male counterparts. Although as educated, modern women they were expected to protest sexual harassment in the workplace, they felt the country's slow legal system would take years to prosecute a case of this nature and they were, in the meantime, only bound to be ostracized as difficult, humorless women.

When I interviewed three female executives in 2010 and two in 2014, all of them noted that teasing is easier to take than the gender discrimination rampant in the garment sector. They related shocking stories about superiors assigning responsibilities to less-qualified male colleagues because they felt that women were not good at such work. These middle class women seem more entangled in a complex web of conventional gender assumptions and capitalist interests, yet the workers' rural roots, migrant status, the FTZ stigma, and the involvement of working class men and city streets make them the targets of government and NGO-sponsored educational workshops on proper responses to sexual harassment. In both cases, something more comprehensive than routine education on sexual harassment seems needed. In the female executives' case, the general climate of gender discrimination and legal disempowerment must change. In the workers' case, improved wages and reward structures could empower them enough economically to take the sexual liberties they experience on the city streets to their relationships and marriages. None of these changes seem achievable without commitment and leadership from the state, civil society, and business sector.

Sexual banter as a site of resistance

Several scholarly writings have questioned the encompassing character of sexual harassment discourses and noted how women may enjoy and seek sexualized banter (Ehrlich and King 1996; Williams et al. 1999). Giuffre (1997) shows that a sexualized work culture can be a consensual coping mechanism in highly stressful professions, such as medicine. Loe (1996) demonstrates how female workers reshaped and negotiated the culture in a restaurant chain that built sexualized behavior into the job description. Synthesizing several such conflicting arguments, Williams et al. (1999) contend that sexual behaviors should be understood in their context and as an interplay of many factors, including individual agency.

While poor pay and the temporary character of their employment prevented them from acquiring tangible symbols of modernity, unrevised versions of global discourses on modern conduct, including recognizing and responding to sexual harassment, were quite liberally disseminated to them through local NGOs. FTZ workers, however, reinterpreted this training in a way that allows them to move between positions as young female FTZ workers who enjoy sexual banter and modern, educated, urban women who are well aware of their right to live without fear of sexual harassment. I acknowledge that public banter on city streets can both empower and exploit, with men being the ones who usually initiate romantic advances. Joking and banter can always move beyond an acceptable form and make women more afraid of enjoying their public space. Even with these risks, ignoring the liberatory potential of sexual banter is a mistake, not only because the banter goes against dominant expectations of behavior for young women, but also because the women workers show agency in contextually deciding which expressions or acts should be pursued as banter and which should be denigrated with sexual harassment vocabulary. Not recognizing this agency opens NGO harassment discourses to the criticism of being elite, middle class, and too Western.

As Setha Low (2000: 237) notes, urban spaces, such as plazas, provide a place to meet friends and find romance as well as a stage for entertainment through the enactment of everyday lives. However, in the case of FTZ streets, the neighbors and the police take it upon themselves to use sexual harassment vocabulary to condemn sexual banter as well as public displays of intimacy. In this context, the FTZ streets provide a forum for gendered and classed struggles over meaning. NGO education on global sexual harassment discourses and FTZ workers' contextual understanding and variable responses produced an interesting contestation over the *proper* use of public spaces and *proper* ways of communicating and interacting among men and women. Public performances of sexual banter represent a meaningful way for working class men and women to articulate their right to city spaces, despite many regulatory forces. By engaging in sexual banter on streets, the women defied both the global harassment discourses espoused by the NGOs and dominant middle class expectations of "respectable, good woman" behavior. Such subaltern resistance registers their resentment of state and global policies that consider them ideal expendable human resources in the service of global capitalist regimes.

Notes

1 "Wariyapola Incident the Vice and the Voice" *Daily Mirror*, August 08, 2014. See more at: www.dailymirror.lk/51648/wariyapola-incident-the-vice-and-the-voice#sthash.jmmAXS4h.dpuf.
2 http://newsfirst.lk/sinhala/2015/09/08
3 At the time of writing, a fundamental rights case is pending for the Supreme Court against the OIC of the Wariyapola police station for illegally arresting the young woman.
4 Quoted in CENWOR document on violence against women. www.cenwor.lk/vaw/english/sexual_harassment.html. Accessed on 06/21/2011.
5 'Sri Lanka, No to Sexual Harassment' http://communicatinglabourrights.wordpress.com/2007/12/17. Accessed on 12/05/2015.
6 'Sri Lanka, No to Sexual Harassment' http://communicatinglabourrights.wordpress.com/2007/12/17. Accessed on 12/05/2015.
7 Quoted in CENWOR document on violence against women. www.cenwor.lk/vaw/english/sexual_harassment.html Accessed on 06/21/2011. This amendment was highly touted by many as a necessary step. However, not many believed that enforcement would be vigorous or easy.
8 Interview, May 2008.
9 All the staff at these four organizations were Sri Lankans, with most coming from the Colombo and Gampaha suburbs, such as Watthala, Mabole, and Negambo. Their Colombo headquarters was also mostly staffed by middle class, English-speaking Sri Lankans with a foreign resident representative or several foreign visitors.
10 Interview, December 2007. Reiterated, almost verbatim, in July 2014. I, however, have never met a woman who said she was afraid to go to work because of sexual harassment.
11 Interview, July 2014. This was a follow up of an initial interview conducted in December 2007.
12 Other youth groups, including university students, also engage in group communication at the beginning of relationships. When I attended the University of Colombo in the 1990s, there was as much direct communication as group communication among

students. Note that although they occupy a "respectable public space," the vast majority of university students also come from rural areas.

13 It is difficult to generalize about the make-up of these male groups except in terms of age. They all tend to be between 20 and 30 years-old. According to rudimentary data collected from women workers who entered into relationships through this mode of communication, the men are in the area because they either work in the FTZ or its vicinity as pavement hawkers, shop salesmen, and bus or three-wheeler drivers, are soldiers on leave, or happen to be visiting friends or relatives. Some young neighborhood men also joined these circles. It seemed as if those who were free in the evening or on the weekends headed toward the junction and influenced others to do likewise.

14 This is the same Kalyani mentioned in the earlier vignette.

15 All these interviews were conducted in December 2008 and some of the same informants, including Jayanthi, recalled the incident in July 2014.

16 Personal communication with Jeanne Marecek, one of the researchers.

References

Barraclough, R. (2006) Tales of Seduction: Factory Girls in Korean Proletarian Literature. *Positions*. 14 (2). pp. 345–371.

Bender, D. (2004) Too Much of Distasteful Masculinity: Historicizing Sexual Harassment in the Garment Sweatshop and Factory. *Journal of Women's History*. 15 (4). pp. 91–116.

Bularzik, M. (1983) Sexual Harassment at the Workplace: Historical Notes. In Green, J. (ed.). *Workers' Struggles, Past and Present: A Radical America Reader*. Philadelphia: Temple University Press. pp. 117–135.

DeVotta, N. (ed.) (2005) *Benedictine Memoirs*. Talangama: JF&I Printers.

Ehrlich, S. and King, R. (1996) Consensual Sex or Sexual Harassment: Negotiating Meaning. In Bergvall, V.L., Bing, J.M. and Freed, A.F. (eds.). *Rethinking Language and Gender Research: Theory and Practice*. London: Longman. pp. 153–172.

Giuffre, P.A. (1997) Labeling Sexual Harassment in Hospitals: A Case Study of Doctors and Nurses. Paper Presented at the Sociologists Against Sexual Harassment Meeting. Toronto, Canada.

Giuffre, P.A. and Williams, C.L. (1994) Boundary Lines: Labeling Sexual Harassment in Restaurants. *Gender and Society*. 8. pp. 378–401.

Gruber, J. (1998) The Impact of Male Work Environments and Organizational Policies on Women's Experiences of Sexual Harassment. *Gender & Society*. 12. pp. 301–320.

Hewamanne, S. (2008) *Stitching Identities in a Free Trade Zone: Gender and Politics in Sri Lanka*. Philadelphia: University of Pennsylvania Press.

Jensen, B. (2005) Bawdy Bodies or Moral Agency?: The Struggle for Identity in Working Class Autobiographies of Imperial Germany. *Biography*. 28 (4). pp. 534–557.

Lerum, K. (2004) Sexuality, Power and Camaraderie in Service Work. *Gender and Society*. 18 (6). pp. 756–776.

Loe, M. (1996) Working for Men – At the Intersection of Power, Gender and Sexuality. *Social Inquiry*. 66. pp. 399–421.

Low, S. (2000) *On the Plaza: The Politics of Public Space and Culture*. Austin: University of Texas Press.

MacKinnon, C.A. (1979) *Sexual Harassment of Working Women: A Case of Sexual Discrimination*. New Haven: Yale University Press.

Narayan, K. (1993) Banana Republics and V.I. Degrees: Rethinking Indian Folklore in a Postcolonial World. *Asian Folklore Studies*. 52. pp. 177–204.

Osella, C. and Osella, F. (1998) Friendship and Flirting: Micro-Politics in Kerala, South India. *Journal of the Royal Anthropological Institute.* 4. pp. 189–206.

Salzinger, L. (2000) Manufacturing Sexual Subjects: "Harassment", Desire and Discipline on a Maquiladora Shop floor. *Ethnography.* 1. pp. 67–92.

Salzinger, L. (2003) *Genders in Production: Making Workers in Mexico's Global Factories.* Berkley: University of California Press.

Uggen, C. and Blackstone, A. (2004) Sexual Harassment as a Gendered Expression of Power. *American Sociological Review.* 69. pp. 64–92.

Williams, C., Giuffre, P., and Dellinger, K. (1999) Sexuality in the Workplace: Organizational Control, Sexual Harassment, and the Pursuit of Pleasure. *Annual Review of Sociology.* 25. pp. 73–93.

Yelvington, K. (1996) Flirting in the Factory. *Journal of Royal Anthropological Institution.* 31. pp. 119–165.

4 "Would good girls read such filth?"

Reading and writing sex among global factory workers

Pointing to some magazines displayed at the entrance to his shop, a Katunayake shop keeper asked: "Would good girls read such filth?" He continued, "I, as an adult, married man, am ashamed to have these things hanging like this in my shop. But this is what they come to the shop to get, and then also buy soap and lentils and things . . . so I have to sell these."

The "filthy" papers he referred to were the colorful weekly tabloid magazines that FTZ women workers considered their favorite reading material. These magazines, which typically carried large pictures of beautiful men and women dressed in skimpy clothing and in "compromising" poses, were sold throughout the FTZ area. The magazines had distinctive titles such as "Snow Roses" (*Hima Rosa*) "Fragrance" (*Suwanda*), "The Virgin" (*Kumari*), "The Bride" (*Manaliya*), "Wife" (*Birinda),* "Prince" (*Kumaraya*), and "Darling" (*Priyadari*). It was commonly said that only "stupid women" bought such magazines and that they were only good for girls in the Zone (*kalape kellanta*). Reading or being seen with one of these weeklies was thought to seriously jeopardize one's reputation as a "good and intelligent woman." For this chapter I will only focus on *Priyadari* as it was the most popular among the workers. While all the other tabloids belonged to the pulp category, *Priyadari* can be termed a pornographic magazine in that it contained sexually explicit material designed for sexual arousal and was sold for profit. It was considered an obscene publication (*asabya*) and proscribed in 2006.

According to Lynda Nead (1993: 148), erotic art's emphasis on form over matter is what differentiates it as high culture and pornography as a low art form. *Priyadari* paid scant attention to form when publishing readers' sexually explicit narratives. Another indicator of pornography is whether the stories were written for sexual arousal. *Priyadari* conveyed the impression that writers had to include sexually explicit details to get published. Thus, for example, even when writers could have simply said, "then we had sex" they went into lengthy details to explain the act. According to these two determinants, *Priyadari* amply qualified as a pornographic publication.

While all the tabloids catered to young people, *Priyadari* especially catered to FTZ workers, who claimed it was among their favorite magazines and bought it from male shop keepers, who looked down on them for buying it. *Priyadari* was composed of articles written by its readers about their romantic and sexual relationships and contained lurid sexual material. There were stories written about FTZ women workers, while some articles were written by workers themselves, based on their own experiences with men.

This chapter shows how FTZ workers read, discussed, and contributed to pornographic magazines and argues that their actions challenge the normative models of sexual behavior dominant Sinhala Buddhist and middle class cultural discourses prescribe for rural women. The workers' contributions and the way they were depicted in others' stories in *Priyadari* evidence an alternative sexual culture that eludes social and psychic controls imposed on them by male and middle class agents and institutions. It is very difficult for women to obtain pornographic material in their native villages. But the special circumstances surrounding the FTZ allows workers a constrained space to obtain and engage in transgressive communication through magazines such as *Priyadari*. Yet this alternative critical space also represents an accommodation to capitalist patriarchy, given that the profit-driven magazine owners commodify women's desires for male consumption. Women workers' engagement with this pornographic material, then, while being critical and transgressive, also ensures the continuation of both sexual and labor exploitation.

That noted, it is important to appreciate the social cultural milieu in which FTZ women workers read and write these stories. According to Sinhala Buddhist culture, good and bad women are constructed in association with the level of adherence to ideal behavioral and sexual norms. As noted in earlier chapters, women expressing sexual desires (and actually fulfilling such desires and then writing about it) are not considered normal. In that sense, this critical space is new and is almost the only public forum women have for (anonymously) expressing transgressive desires and activities that enunciate an alternative sexual subculture. In the previous two chapters I discussed how women did not use the direct Sinhala word for desire (*ashawa*) in their everyday lives. The stories in *Priyadari*, however, contained words like *ashawa, sapa* (pleasure), and *unusuma* (heat). At the same time, women evidenced deference to cultural norms by withholding their names and using pseudonyms when writing for *Priyadari*. This critical space, therefore, marks a point where women's struggle for sexual agency find voice within certain limitations.

The first section of this chapter recounts several stories from the magazine to show how FTZ workers express alternative sexual norms. The second section analyzes how women reconcile their conflictual feelings about transgressing deeply internalized values by constructing an ambiguous space wherein they justify reading pornography by claiming it compensates for their lack of education. I do this by focusing on their boarding house magazine reading sessions, where women read the stories together and discussed them in detail. By focusing on their secretive magazine reading sessions within village homes, I also show how they operate as agents who expose village women to new values. The chapter further discusses how two alternate magazines designed to promote ideal "good romance" befitting good FTZ girls challenged the likes of *Priyadari* and allowed the workers to use both varieties to negotiate their own notions of intimacy, sex, and marriage. I ultimately argue that considering the multiple hegemonic forces that seek to constrain women, consuming and contributing to pornographic magazines like *Priyadari* is emancipatory.

Priyadari

There were at least two magazines that carried pornographic stories but for ease of analysis I focus only on *Priyadari*. The main reason for doing so is the magazine's popularity among the FTZ workers and the frequency with which it published workers' writings.[1] The magazine was published on a small budget and depended almost entirely on readers' writings to fill its pages. Furthermore, there was little editing done on the writings sent in. Writers were encouraged to express how they felt about sensitive issues, and their writings were published uncensored. The stories featured hidden aspects of Sri Lankan social life that were rarely taken up by the mainstream media, such as widespread domestic and child abuse, incest, rape, and flagrant discrimination and police brutality against poor, marginalized groups. The articles were written in everyday language and were replete with grammatical and stylistic mistakes. When people wrote about bad in-laws or lovers who spurned them, they used abusive terms and swore and cursed in equal measure. This was quite a contrast to the formal, almost scholarly, writing style that the mainstream magazines and newspapers demanded from contributors.

Priyadari apparently accepted any article, provided it centered on some aspect of sexuality.[2] This acceptance, regardless of the language used, made it a fine forum for marginalized groups, especially garment factory workers and soldiers. The magazine provided them a space to write about their relationships, release pent up emotions, and boast about their casual attitude toward love and sex. There were pages devoted to various topics, with titles like, "Scattered Flower Petals" ("how I lost my virginity before marriage"), "My Wedding Night", "A Broken Relationship", "What We Did Before Marriage", "How We Eloped from Home," and "A Secret I Can't Tell Anybody" (on adulterous relationships), etc. As suggested by these titles, the articles often contained lurid sexual descriptions and graphic details. Each page was adorned with semi-naked men and women in different poses of sexual intimacy. The sections regularly carried FTZ workers' stories or stories written about the FTZ workers by jilted lovers, former friends, or in-laws.

Stories, writers, and readers

Mainstream newspapers and magazines claim that sheltered young rural women, once at the FTZ, get trapped by urban males in relationships that cause them many problems. According to these writers, young women are victims of unscrupulous men. When such writings blame the workers, it is not for desiring sex, but for lacking the strength to resist men's advances. They also assert that women get into such relationships because they are fascinated with urban life and are lonely, not because they seek to fulfil sexual desires.

Priyadari had a singularly different approach to premarital sex. More than half of the magazine was devoted to stories of premarital sex, and the paper was non-judgmental about the accounts readers sent in. Consequently, some stories portrayed garment factory workers in ways that were different from the stories published in the mainstream press. While the latter never talked about women getting into relationships because they needed sexual gratification, *Priyadari's* stories, written mostly by jilted lovers, portrayed FTZ workers as sexually assertive and, in some cases, over sexed, scheming, manipulative women who would cruelly abandon men after they fulfilled their financial and sexual needs. They also compared FTZ women to other young women who have not been to the city and celebrated the latter's ignorance of sexual matters. It was also striking that members of the armed forces and police contributed many such stories. Written in anger and pain, they probably exaggerated women's instrumental behavior and cruelty. However, the frequency with which such stories appeared in these magazines and their credibility[3] warrant a careful analysis of their content.

In *Priyadari*, it was women, who more often than not, initiated relationships (and sometimes even sexual activities) through friends or by writing letters to men. In these accounts women almost always enjoyed sex and in some cases educated the men on sexual matters. These women did not hesitate to leave a relationship when it became undesirable and showed much creative capability in disappearing without a trace in the FTZ area by changing factories and boarding houses. There were several stories about women getting married just to obtain the marriage certificate, so they could obtain their Employee's Provident Fund and gratuity payments, after which they simply vanished. In one case a woman lied about having made a vow to abstain from sex with her newly married husband until the gods grant her requests. One woman was said to disappear right after exiting the marriage registrar's office and, according to the account, the husband continued to roam the FTZ area looking for his wife. Most male writers, including military personnel, portrayed themselves as victims and portrayed their ex-girlfriends as unscrupulous and skilled cheaters. This situation contains an inversion of another stereotype: the members of the armed forces and police as the strong, unemotional corrupters of young rural women. At the same time, it says as much about the image of the "ideal man," given that the men here were blaming women for sexual transgressions, thereby suggesting that coming across as being sexually non-motivated was important for men as well. Especially since many such men expected the female readers to sympathize with them and start correspondence through the magazine, this portrayal of themselves as sexually non-motivated was of strategic importance.

According to NGO staff members, FTZ workers got entangled with military and police personnel mainly for the strong sense of security these men brought to their insecure and unprotected lives. It is this same patriarchal relationship that makes them victims of physical abuse, deceit, and abandonment. There are numerous stories of military men and policemen seducing and leaving women pregnant and in shame. It is usually the women who cry foul. But in the *Priyadari* stories men also talked about having their lives destroyed because the women betrayed them. The vocabulary these men typically used to express anger and sadness was very similar to what mainstream media used when discussing how evil urban men betrayed and abandoned gullible FTZ workers. One *Priyadari* story written by a military man continued as follows: "She told me fairy tales to make me get lost in a butterfly world and then she darkened my life." If the gendered terms are changed in the following sentence to say, "I thought I was in love with an innocent girl but actually loved a whore: now because of that whore an innocent life[4] is being destroyed," it is almost identical to what one read when women discussed cheating men. Most of these stories by men were written in what is commonly known as "emotional" or "women's language" that portrayed a vulnerable side to security personnel, which was different from the strong image FTZ women workers typically associated with them.

The accounts men and women contributed can be grouped into three broad categories according to their content. First, and the most prevalent, were women's stories that bared all and demanded and pleaded with readers to understand that they too have desire*s* (*ashawan*) that need to be fulfilled. The second category comprised stories of women that depicted "transgressive sexual behavior" even while they adhered to certain ideal family and gender norms. These stories expressed intense struggles and deep guilt. The third category contained stories written by men. While some men wrote to boast about their sexual exploits, the majority wrote to express hateful feelings toward women who had wronged them.

In a 2000 issue of *Priyadari*[5] "H from Rathnapura" wrote about a FTZ worker that was published under the section titled "A Broken Relationship." According to the author, an army soldier, he met Sitha after she responded to his letter in *Priyadari*'s personal advertisement page. Sitha was a FTZ garment factory worker, and the author was stationed at an army camp in Vavuniya. When the author asked Sitha to meet him at a bus terminal she readily agreed. After a long conversation over a soft drink he invited her to go to a movie. He says that "She happily came and while in the theatre we engaged in oral sex. Afterwards I asked her whether she would go to a rooming house in Avissawelle with me. We went there and spent two days there. She did not go to work during those days. For almost two years after that we met every time I was on vacation, and we had sex at different hotels in the country." He includes lurid details in describing their sexual escapades and portrays both of them as sexually aggressive. After about two years he stopped getting letters from her and therefore started looking for her. "I wrote to her again and again and went to her house and her friends' houses to look for her. But she could not be found. They said she had gone back to Colombo but did not know how to find her. After several months I got to know through mutual friends that she was living with another man in a FTZ boarding room. I could not bear the way she took an innocent war hero (*ranaviruva*) like me and then played with my life until she got tired and just threw me away."

This story portrays a woman who is not afraid to make decisions for herself and enjoy life. She is not a clinging FTZ worker who merely engages in sex to keep the man from looking elsewhere, or puts up with an exploitative relationship because she thinks she now has no choice but try and get married to the man she had sex with. This definitely is not a woman who is governed by middle class sexual norms. I encountered several such *Priyadari* stories in which women happily engaged in sexual activities and then distanced themselves without explanation.

K of Nagarkovil Army camp published a story under the section "A Sad Story of an Army Soldier" that closely resembles the anxiety-ridden creative writings published in mainstream magazines.[6] According to the story, the author and his former girlfriend fell in love while they were in secondary school. After leaving school K joined the armed forces while his girlfriend became a garment factory worker. In the beginning they were happy and they met in her boarding house whenever they could. But he started noticing a change within a short time. Once he went to her boarding house only to see her returning in the car of a factory official and smelling of alcohol. He asked her to marry him but she wanted to work for a few more years before getting married. Soon people began relating to him unsavory accounts about her but he "was blinded by love" and did not believe the rumors. But then one of her closest friends told him that his girlfriend went to hotels with different men. He was saddened and stopped going to see her. One day he saw her walking along the road and a street vendor told him that she was a prostitute waiting for a customer. He confronted her and she confessed to becoming a sex worker and told him that her quest for wealth and comforts ended in her becoming a sex worker. He still loved her and offered to marry her but she refused, saying that she was not worthy of him. About six months later she went to Kuwait to work as a housemaid.

Though the story follows a familiar trope of village women getting into trouble in immoral urban areas, what makes this account interesting is the woman's refusal to marry her former lover. From his perspective she is a prostitute and needs his help to become a respectable woman through marriage. But she chose to change her life by changing the geographical location and taking up a better paying job. Domestic service in a Middle Eastern country is not an easy choice given the many pitfalls women face in such unfamiliar environs. Choosing this difficult option instead of marrying her former boyfriend evidences a strong character and non-normative thinking.

A story written by "U of Pollonnaruwa," under the feature heading "Our Honeymoon Night," compared a rural woman who had never migrated with a FTZ worker and extolled the virtues of the former for adhering to cultural norms rooted in innocence and virginity.[7] According to the story, the writer got engaged to a FTZ worker named Geeta, following a marriage proposal. Two days before the wedding ceremony news reached him that Geeta had eloped with another man. He describes his feelings as follows: "I could not bear the pain and the humiliation. Even though many people look at garment sisters with squinted eyes, I had never done so. But I don't even want to write about what I thought of them after this incident." Both families, however, urged him to marry Geeta's cousin so that the wedding could go ahead as planned. Thus, Renu, an eighteen year old village woman, married him just two days after the arrangement was made. He says that he looks up to her as a goddess for saving him from suicidal thoughts following Geeta's elopement.

Writing about their honeymoon night he celebrates her ignorance of sexual activities and her reluctance for physical intimacy. At first he was angry with her objections and questioned her. "She looked at me with tearful eyes and said, 'Please be a brother to me. I have come with you after leaving my parents and family because I have seen your sadness. I did not know that you are going to do something like this.' At this I became tearful too. Can you believe that my little bride who was 18 at the time did not know what people do after getting married? You will think that my little girl is a stupid woman. No. She has passed her O/L exam with five passes and three credits. But she has not gone the wrong way. I had intercourse for the first time after marriage too. But I learned these things from books and friends. But my little girl did not. Today my precious girl knows those things very well. The bed is like a heaven to us. I haven't ever raised my voice to my god."[8] At the end he thanks Geeta for eloping with someone else and letting him have a good wife like Renu.

Even though the writer was upset at first, Renu's reluctance on her wedding night not only inspired kindness but high esteem for her "moral superiority." Even though he does not use the exact words, what he celebrates in this article is the "innocence" from sexual knowledge – the most sought after quality in a young Sinhala Buddhist woman.[9] Geeta's actions are in complete contrast to her cousin Renu, who agrees to marry a man she had never thought of liking but does so because her parents wanted it. Because she was leaving her job to get married Geeta was able to claim her accumulated EPF, ETF payments and a substantial factory gratuity. She had chosen her own partner and, taking what was due to her from the employer, went away with her boyfriend to start a new life.

While such stories depict strong, desiring women and contradict the familiar picture that FTZ workers are weak victims, there are stories written by women that convey the complex conflicts that riddle their lives. FTZ working women straddle different cultural discourses in the globalized transnational spaces in which they work and the patriarchal villages to which they are bound in many ways. While the stories written by women for *Priyadari* unabashedly reveal their sexual escapades, they also reveal intense anxieties and subtly plead with readers to understand and sympathize with their positions.

While writing about their premarital sexual experiences or how one cheated a trusting boyfriend by being with another, they did not blame their partners for their actions. Rather the stories revealed how their physical desires were aroused by a different way of looking or touching. They also confessed to deep emotions of love and tenderness toward their lovers. K from Hingurakgoda, writing in 2005 about her life as a FTZ worker under the heading "Things that have Happened to Me,"[10] discussed how she went on a pleasure trip with her factory friends. Although she had a boyfriend at that time, she liked the conductor/cleaner of the bus they hired for the trip. "He had such sexy (*wal*) eyes. I fell for it," she explained. They then spent most of the day and night flirting, kissing, fondling, and engaging in sex. As she noted, "We had sex with our clothes on. So you know what we did." Next day by the time the bus reached Katunayake, they were inseparably bonded. Twice thereafter he visited her at the boarding house and they had sex. Once, she said, "he bent me over a chair," which she found especially exciting. When he came by the third time her boyfriend was there and a big fight ensued. Her boyfriend and the boarding owner's son together beat the new guy until he fled bleeding, and they then proceeded to scold her in filth and beat her. The other women in the boarding house chased them away and took her inside.

But then she learned that her jilted boyfriend had tried to commit suicide by jumping in front of a train. When they all ran to the railroad, they saw him lying near the rail tracks weeping and drunkenly yelling about her 'whore-like behavior." She felt sad and ashamed and lost all good sense, resulting in her running back to the boarding house shouting that she was going to commit suicide. She grabbed the kerosene bottle from the common kitchen and poured it all over her. But the women who ran behind her prevented her from setting herself on fire. Throughout this story she maintained a light hearted, humorous tone. Soon she left the factory and the boarding house and stayed with her family in the village for five months. She then found a job at a different FTZ factory and residence at a different boarding house. She dumped both boyfriends and found another. She ended the story by noting that she still remembered the fun she had with the second guy she met on the bus. "Some days, when I am looking into the night, enjoying the cool breeze and moon light, I still remember his sexy eyes," she confessed in the very last line.

In this instance the woman recounted her experience with much bravado, although she did struggle with her own "bad" behavior and tried to commit suicide. She also managed her reputation by taking a few months break in the village and starting anew. It is interesting that when writing under a pseudonym and a few years removed from the experience, women are capable of vividly expressing desires and pleasure. This particular woman's story revealed another intriguing aspect of FTZ romances, which is that many workers prefer not to have sex with boyfriends they expected to marry. This is a strategy to balance the need for romance while meeting cultural expectations of being pure at marriage. Women feared that their boyfriends would revile them as bad, immoral women if they had sex before marriage. This may be why one heard of some women engaging in spontaneous sex with near strangers, with whom they did not envision a future.

Unlike the above story, women's anonymous accounts are often couched in patriarchal terms. Some women noted the failure of their fathers, boyfriends or husbands to perform their patriarchal duties as the reason for their transgressions. Women who talked about their premarital sexual adventures repeatedly noted how much they loved their partners and how much they were looking forward to becoming these men's brides, wives and the mothers of their children. Many urged the paper to publish the story quickly so they could share it with and convey their love to their partners.

There were also some articles through which women pleaded for forgiveness from parents and siblings for their transgressions. Some women wrote about pre-marital sexual activities only to reveal at the end that the partner abandoned them. Such accounts usually ended with the women reminding partners of all the pleasures they shared and asking the men to come back to them. In some other cases, after describing a premarital sexual relationship that ended bitterly, women asked kind-hearted, sympathetic men to write to them.[11] In most such cases they invited soldiers disabled in the civil war to write to them. Even though most of these women celebrated their sexual adventures in writing, they still seemed to consider losing their virginity akin to a physical handicap that prevented them from marrying a physically complete man.

It is important to note that among the 110 issues of *Priyadari* that I analyzed for this chapter (and other issues I read over the years), I have never found a story dealing with homosexual love among FTZ workers. I, however, found one male homosexual love story among the issues analyzed and an account of lesbian desire and betrayal.[12] This does not say that there are no such relationships among FTZ workers; rather it suggests that writing for *Priyadari* is more of a heterosexual leisure activity whereby women's transgressions get commodified. Another interesting fact is that although I have conducted research in the FTZ for years, I have not met a worker who claimed to have written a story to the paper. Women used pseudonyms while writing to *Priyadari*, thereby showing the hold that dominant cultural norms still have over transgressing women. This is much more telling when we consider how FTZ workers proudly display their names with their creative writings in magazines like *Dabindu* and *Niveka*.

Reading community and education

While only a few FTZ working women wrote stories to *Priyadari*, many more read the pornographic stories in boarding rooms. The workers admitted that they read *Priyadari* for juicy sexual accounts (*pani keli*). Writings on women's romance reading have already established that it fulfils very real emotional needs while representing a resistance, however limited, to patriarchal values (Modleski 1982; Radway 1984). Reading *Priyadari*, while it no doubt fulfilled emotional needs and provided an escape from their difficult lives, also provided a chance for FTZ women workers to defy metaphysical barriers placed on their actions by patriarchal sexual norms.

Priyadari was a familiar sight at boarding houses – on tables, under the mattresses or on the floor. Usually when an issue first became available at the boarding house women read it as a group, with one person reading a story aloud while others listened. Usually these were lively, interactive sessions and as the reading went on women expressed their opinions on a particular story or its sexual contents to much laughter and gestures of embarrassment. The women kept magazines under their beds for weeks and individual women read selected issues whenever they had a little free time. These selected issues or articles almost always contained extensive sexual details. However, they always explained their continuing interest in terms of the insights the story provided them or someone else.[13]

Many workers considered the magazine educational as it provided much needed sexual knowledge to FTZ workers. One woman said, "If people read the stories in the magazines seriously they won't fall into the traps out there. They would know how to deal with a situation." A spokeswoman for the Women's Bureau expressed exactly the opposite sentiment by saying, "If they read books and good magazines like *Tharuni* and *Sirikatha* rather than reading papers like *Priyadari, Suwanda* and *Birinda* they will be better equipped to deal with the problems they face in the urban environment." NGO staff members also complained that the workers read magazines like *Priyadari* rather than reading good material.

Fifteen workers were present in the room when we discussed the magazine and all of them agreed that reading material such as *Priyadari* was a great way to obtain information about issues shrouded in secrecy in Sinhala Buddhist culture. "Parents, schools or the government should give us knowledge or let us learn on our own. I don't think women should get married without being informed of sexual issues," one woman said. Another woman narrated an experience of a former FTZ worker who learned what to do if there was no blood on the bed sheets on the wedding night (at first sexual intercourse) from a story in *Priyadari*. "My friend remembered that the woman in the story sat down and pressed herself on the bed sheets. My friend also realized that if she kept lying down there was no chance that she could prove her virginity so she did the same and she was saved from shame." Many women claimed that they now know how to discern good men from bad men and to read the actions and facial expressions of their boyfriends, thanks to *Priyadari*.

As explicated earlier, the FTZ experience gave them a chance to escape some of the social codes surrounding sexual behavior. Rather than getting married right after high school they now experienced difficult but relatively free lives in a vibrant, urban social space that allowed more room for expressing physical desires. New workers saw and heard about other women's romances and adventures and within a few months of entering the FTZ they too roamed around arm in arm with new-found boyfriends. It is this unusual number of couples in the area that inspired the derogatory term "*prema kalape*" or love zone to refer to the FTZ and its immediate surroundings. Whether they engaged in premarital sexual activities or not, all women tried to publicly claim that their relationships were non-sexual. It was perhaps these public denials that prompted them to write to the magazine under pseudonyms. Women who did not write their own stories celebrated the ones they shared in the rooms. And it was during such times that women most strongly expressed their anger, frustration, and resistance to dominant cultural formations.

Women almost always applauded when a female protagonist in a story managed to escape an abusive relationship and especially appreciated when women wrote about coming to the FTZ or going to the Middle East as a way to get away from unreasonable parents or abusive partners. While they celebrated women's strong characters, they ridiculed men who expressed too much sadness about a broken relationship. Women got angry and cursed at men who abused their partners; and they were joyous when bad things happened to such men in the end.

They were also angry at women who stuck with abusive men claiming that they did so "for the children's sake" or "for love's sake." According to many workers, it was fear and lethargy that prevented such writers from taking advantage of the opportunities available to women, and dumping abusive men. There are many gaps, excesses, contradictions and ambiguities in the stories they read and this required them to speculate and graft scenarios to such accounts. Their additions to these gray areas and endings were usually within the parameters that the dominant culture allowed but sometimes combined culturally accepted solutions with extreme fantasies. Women frequently expressed dissatisfaction with the endings in the stories, because they were usually either too sad or shocking, and so they collectively created their own finales.

The workers usually got angry with women who callously cheated on unsuspecting partners who did not mistreat them. However, there were also a few workers who tried to read between the lines about what drove women toward another man. These women laughingly suggested that men should not think that everything is fine just because they provided material comforts for women. Lack of interest in sexual activities, not spending time with the family, and lack of tender, loving care were noted as good reasons for women to pursue other relationships. But others demonized women who cheated on non-abusive, honest, and hardworking men.

Their friends laughed when women who did not have boyfriends in the FTZ were found reading *Priyadari* alone. Urging a relatively new worker to start a relationship with an admirer, one woman said, "Otherwise you will have to live your life reading *Priyadari*." The way she used the language conveyed how *Priyadari* provides sexual contentment and knowledge about life. While women readily agreed that pornographic stories in *Priyadari* provided pleasure, they tried to understand their infatuation by creating an ambiguous space in which they emphasized its educational function.

As to why women have to create this new set of meanings to understand one of their favorite leisure activities becomes clear when we consider the context in which they read the stories in *Priyadari* or write for *Priyadari*. Though there are several publications like *Priyadari*, they mostly cater to a male clientele. Women workers talked about how difficult it was to find a copy of *Priyadari* in their villages. Even if they did find one, reading it without arousing a big furor was a struggle. Many women had not even seen such magazines before coming to the FTZ. Several women said that they had seen at least one issue of *Priyadari* or a similar magazine while in the villages. Two women reported being severely reprimanded after being caught reading such magazines, and one woman said she was beaten. During a focus group conducted in July 2015, all the participants again said that it is still impossible to obtain such magazines in their villages and that they believed this was the case for men as well.

The extent to which women's writings in *Priyadari* angered men also shows the critical power of women's pornographic writings. For example, A. Wijesinghe from the Kalmadu army camp[14] severely reprimanded a woman writer by noting in his response that if he was her husband he would insert about ten bottles into her vagina until they came out of her mouth. Evidencing the connection between suppressing women's desire and patriarchy, several other responses by men (mostly military personnel) suggested using haberano peppers (*kochchi kottanna*) to curb women's unsatiable desires (*gaaya*). Clearly the unmarried women who enjoyed sex and boasted about it in writing incensed such men's sense of masculinity, so much so that they wanted to put women in their place by using sexual violence.

Taking sex stories to villages

As stated earlier, middle classes and males look down upon FTZ workers for leaving their villages and living alone in the city. They were talked about in everyday discourses as immoral women and "Juki pieces" ("Juki" in reference to the name of the sowing machine women used in the factories and "pieces" to refer to the specific part they attached to a garment as part of the assembly line process). The flip side of this stigmatization of migrant workers is the idealization of women who did not migrate to urban areas to work as this sheltered them among family and community and, therefore, they were considered more respectable. FTZ workers took revenge on these moral advocates by discreetly sharing their new knowledge with village women. Many women at the boarding houses confessed to taking at least one copy of *Priyadari* home and sharing it with younger village women in the privacy of their rooms. While they took copies of *Priyadari* home secretly, they were less fearful when taking other tabloids such as *Suwanda* or *Himarosa*, which occupied an ambiguous space between being silly youth papers and unsuitable reading matter. What they feared most about taking *Priyadari* home was that village elders would blame them for corrupting younger non-migrant women.

FTZ women who constantly emphasized the magazine's educational value, however, felt the need to educate village women about worldly matters. "Some of these women are from very poor families. But they are so ignorant about life that they fear taking up a FTZ job in Colombo. When they get to know there are readings that educate us it makes them less fearful. And they also like to enjoy life like the women who write to *Priyadari*," one woman said. According to Disna, another FTZ worker, "It helps young women to know it is common to have desires and also to know it is not the end of life if that [losing her virginity] happens to her." Disna had persuaded her uncle's daughter to come to the FTZ by talking to her about *Priyadari* reading sessions. "She wanted to get to know that life," Disna declared and then quickly added "not the sex [life] but the reading and learning part."

Once when visiting a worker's village in Anuradhapura, a district located 200 miles from Colombo, I was also present when a worker, Mala, showed a copy of *Priyadari* to four village women. These women had been pleading with Mala the whole day to show them the magazine. Mala took pleasure in holding it back but kept dropping hints as to how good the issue was. In fact, this particular issue contained two lurid stories and when we read the paper at night the younger women expressed surprise, embarrassment, and excitement. I also detected their hidden hopes for a fast paced, adventurous life being aroused. Thus while the FTZ work facilitates a contestatory feminist act such as reading and writing to pornographic magazines, the latter quietly facilitates the migration of more young women to the Katunayake area.

Obscene papers, divine flowers, and digital porn

Debate on pornography is usually linked with the debate on high and low cultural forms. Pornography is a forum where "vulgar" pleasures and "coarse" tastes, so banished from the middle class notions of pure culture, find voice. According to Bourdieu, those who consume such "vulgar" and "coarse" pleasures assume lower positions within the social hierarchy (1984). FTZ women reading the magazine, therefore, is not only a gendered critique of patriarchal norms, it is also a class critique in which working women refused to be constrained by middle class dictates of high and low cultural forms.

Not surprisingly the people in power did not let these transgressions and critiques proceed unhindered. In 2007, when the civil war was at its most intense, the government decided to crack down on printed porn (*asabya prakashana*). This caused *Priyadari* to be proscribed as an obscene publication. For about two years I could not see *Priyadari* copies out in the open, although women confided that they were still being sold as wrapping paper for lunch packets. By 2009, Pleasure Publishers had started printing a magazine named *A to Z*, which had the same format as *Priyadari* without photos of half-naked embracing couples on the cover. Rather cleverly, they had photos of a woman and a man inserted near the letter A and Z, respectively, thereby indicating how things proceeded from *A to Z* – from looks to sexual intercourse. I became aware of the meaning of the cover art during a focus group in 2010, only after workers alerted me to it. While old copies of *Priyadari* still circulated in boarding houses, workers now avidly read *A to Z*, *Bambara* and *Suwanda*. In 2010 the government again went after porn, but this time it was digital porn. By 2010, mobile phones and cheaper internet services were freely available, and men who used their phones to upload on youtube compromising footage of young girlfriends without their consent had outraged the government. This crackdown did not affect FTZ workers much, as they did not have smart phones or own computers.

As of July 2015, I was still to meet a FTZ worker who owned a smart phone or computer. A few women noted that their boyfriends or family members had smart phones. In 2015, a boarding house owner said that workers buy smart phones and laptops as soon as they get their first salary. Yet none of the about 75 women in that boarding house owned or had access to such items. Interviews and participant observation at boarding houses also made clear that these workers did not have easy internet access. Considering that by 2012 only 18 percent of Sri Lanka's population had internet access, it is not surprising that FTZ workers are yet to become familiar with the medium.[15]

The 2006 attempt seeking to curb access to obscene publications and the 2010 measures to curb digital porn had little impact on FTZ workers. A more serious challenge to their reading and writing pornographic material came in the form of two other magazines that also targeted FTZ women. It was in 2005 that I first heard that women were also reading two other magazines that some claimed were now their favorite reading material. These magazines contained serialized novels and they promoted viewpoints that countered those of Pleasure Publishers. The women depicted in the new publications resisted male advances and sexual urges, saving themselves for "good, moral" men with whom they went to temples and engaged in charity. This new model for 'good romance' was presented as part of modernity and encouraged women to adopt particular consumption practices and leisure activities. Interviews revealed that a personal rivalry between the owners of Pleasure Publishers and an editor had caused the latter to start Divine Flower Publishers, which chose to distinguish itself by promoting the "ideal romance."

Sandarajini and *Bhavana*, both published by Divine Flower, presented an ideal through their serialized novels that I call "good romance." For instance, in a 2001 *Priyadari* issue a FTZ worker noted how she took revenge on her unfaithful boyfriend: "After that, I decided to sleep with the first man who invited me to do so. When Ajith asked me to go to a room with him, I happily agreed." A serialized novel in a 2006 issue of *Bhavana* described a couple's physical intimacy thus: "He kissed her forehead, and they hung onto each other for a minute or so. And then he distanced her lovingly and said, 'Little sister, you should go now. Mother must be waiting for you. It is not good to go home too late.' Her heart swelled with much pride and love for him that tears filled her eyes. He too looked at her with tear-filled eyes as she moved toward the bus stand." A story in a 2006 *Priyadari* issue recounted how a factory owner's son had sex with the story's author and two other garment workers on the same day; a 2009 *Sandarajini* story depicted a couple going to the temple and distributing religious shawls (*sil redi*) to elderly women.

Many *Sandarajini* stories also depicted married protagonists leading blissful domestic lives. The stories educated FTZ workers on how ideal relationships lead to ideal marriages with couples exchanging loving endearments, sharing household duties, and practicing good citizenship. This education also encouraged workers to desire new patterns of consumption and leisure activities. In several serialized novels, the female protagonists expressed a desire to get pregnant, wear a "preggie" gown, and walk hand-in-hand with their husbands. For couples, taking a walk every evening for exercise and as part of a bonding experience is hardly part of normal married life especially for working class couples, whose work and living arrangements do not facilitate such interactions. Yet the stories encourage workers to pursue such activities as part of the modernity they seek to achieve through transnational factory work.

Sandarajini projected the ideal romance as a compromise between arranged marriage and romantic love. While falling in love is celebrated as the most pure and authentic emotional experience, the ensuing relationships are shaped through self-control, extreme sacrifices, and long commitment to the partner – sometimes over family and community objections. Attaining parental blessings through hardship is thus celebrated as the ultimate joy of romantic love. Men's actions also reiterate patriarchal values, highlighting the father's right to decide his daughter's future. While *Priyadari* articles were mostly written by readers, *Bhavana* and *Sandarajani* stories were authored by the company owner Sujeewa Prassanara-chchi. These carefully orchestrated romances provided women with different images and vocabulary through which to articulate their own notions of love, marriage, intimacy, and domesticity. A person associated with both companies told me that when Sujeewa was with Pleasure Publishers, he wrote some of the sexually explicit stories published in *Priyadari*. When I talked to Sujeewa's clos-est associate (despite repeated requests Sujeewa did not grant an interview), he vehemently denied it: "Sujeewa would never write such filthy stories. He is a good, Buddhist gentleman who has a virtuous wife and two beautiful children. He left *Priyadari* because he wants to create a different picture for our garment factory girls."[16]

Managing reputations

After considering the styles of both magazines, we must see how FTZ women actually received and interpreted their content. While I have interviewed women workers over the past 15 years on various aspects of the FTZ, I interviewed them in 2008 and 2014 to specifically learn more about their reading practices. Although women foregrounded their love for Divine Flower magazines, I quickly noticed that *Priyadari* (titled *A to Z* in 2014) magazines were also lying about in inconspicuous places. Soon workers started opening up and said they liked to read both publications. Clearly, they now did not read *Priyadari* (*A to Z*) as openly as they did earlier. *Sandarajani* and *Bhavana*, which were supposedly promoting a "cleaner" image, had sparked conflicts and struggles over individual performances of respectability. Notwithstanding their actual preference, when asked by outsid-ers, the women were compelled to note the "good romance" magazines as their favorite reading material so as to manage their already precarious reputations.

Ruwani explained her attachment to both types of magazines: "*Priyadari* stories are realistic. That is what happens within most relationships. *Sandarajini* stories are like dreams. They are beautiful and after you read a story you can dream about such good things happening to you. But many of us know that they are just fanta-sies." Among FTZ workers, the images were not always whole-heartedly absorbed but appear to evoke a desire toward "good romance." A woman who desires a "good romance" would have to toe the line with regard to "respectable behavior."

In 2014 I discussed the two magazines with about 15 workers. Chamari said, "Both magazines are good for us. We can learn from both. *Priyadari* shows us how it really is, while *Sandarajini* shows us how it should be." Nisali noted, "*San-darajini* stories are kind of depressing as we know that those romances are not for the likes of us. In a way, *Priyadari* stories make us feel better because we have not fallen as much as the writers of those stories." However circuitously expressed, women seemed to take advantage of both magazines to articulate their diverse positions in relation to gendered sexual regimes. They could use *Sandarajini* to tell outsiders that they are reading "silly yet decent and acceptable" magazines;

and they seem adept at using the *Priyadari* sexual stories to claim they are not as "morally debased" as the anonymous women who authored them.

Evidencing their awareness of the capitalistic interests behind the production of such stories, Nirosha said, "Women who write to *Priyadari* write as if premarital sex is great. The reason is that women know they have to write that way, or else their accounts will not get published." During the ensuing conversation, however, many women said that *Priyadari* stories depict common realities, and noted that even though the magazine did not encourage women to write about all sides of a story, it still provided an important service by making a public forum available.

When I noted that I planned to interview the people associated with both publishing companies, Nilanthi, an NGO worker, angrily declared, "These magazines are such a problem! Even if they go hungry, some women need their magazines. At least *Priyadari* is 10 rupees. *Sandarajini* is 60 rupees. Why can't they see that these businessmen are making a killing here?"

I related this conversation at one of the boarding houses. Chamari said, "We know these are commercial products. Is she suggesting that we should not buy anything and produce our own things? We need some happiness in our difficult lives. It is good sometimes to forget everything and go to a dream world. And then, of course, *Priyadari* stories bring us back to earth," she laughed.

These conversations showed that the women workers sympathize with men of their socio-economic background. Rather than representing an uncritical acceptance of idealized ways to desire and love, their reading practices make selective, practical use of available avenues to express sexual lives and leisure time engaged in what I term "conscious fantasizing" – they fantasize about ideal romances and marriages knowing that they probably will not materialize. In the same way that they express dissatisfaction with transnational production for not allowing them to achieve sustainable livelihoods, the discussions surrounding these magazines, especially *Sandarajini*, criticize the romantic ideals presented to them in a sociocultural milieu that makes them impossible.

Pornography, feminism, and alternative voices

According to anti-pornography feminists, pornography objectifies women and leads to violence against women (Luff 2001). For them pornography is constitutive of women's oppression and could not be a vehicle through which women express opposition to patriarchal domination. Anti-censorship feminists, however, have shown that pornography is just a representation of women's oppression and indeed can be liberatory in some instance such as feminist erotica and gay and lesbian pornography (Luff 2001). Hence they argue that the answer to sexual oppression and violence against women is not to censor pornography but to empower women to explore openly their own interests and pleasures in the realm of the sexual (Segal 1993: 5–21). FTZ workers reading and writing sexually explicit narratives of female desire and sexual activities is thus an emancipatory feminist act, though it remains in the margins and necessitates that women use secrecy, anonymity, and the safety of the FTZ to engage in it. Divine Flower Publications constrain and complicate this critical space available to them. Women workers did understand their vulnerable position within sexual narratives and realities. They were aware of powerful interests that may be shaping and co-opting women's narrative spaces. Moreover, they understood the critical potency of a limited public forum such as *Priyadari.*

Reading pornography in the safety of their rooms and the FTZ area does not change the socio-cultural circumstances that necessitated women to write to such magazines and to read them covertly. Their oppositional act, though having much potential for transformational politics, usually does not lead to collective reflections that encourage political activism, and it thus represents another aspect of these women's temporary hiatus in the city.

None of this belies the fact that women reading and writing pornography represent an alternative voice. And this voice is issued in a context where young unmarried women are supposed to be naïve of sexual knowledge until marriage and strict norms govern women's sexual behavior. When women, who have already transgressed the ideal by migrating to urban areas, create and participate in a sexual subculture that emphasized reading and writing explicit narratives of sexual desire and sexual activities, it represents a conscious oppositional act to the constraining dominant cultural ideals. Consequently, this voice is emancipatory, within which women explored and celebrated hitherto forbidden pleasures. But the voice was constrained by its expressed longings for heterosexual family life. Yet, FTZ workers reading pornography does undermine the normative models of sexual behavior for unmarried, rural Sri Lankan women and thus represents a contestation. If we ignore these new practices and voices because they do not transform the existing structures, we will be succumbing to the dictates of those agents and institutions that seek to regiment our sexual lives.

Notes

1 The magazine now appears under a different name, *A to Z*. However, workers continue to refer to stories in *Priyadari* and also exchange old editions whenever they run into copies.
2 The outfit publishing the paper conducted its operations in secrecy. For instance, the paper provided the names of its editors and photographers but gave no phone numbers. I obtained a cellular phone number for one of its personnel with utmost difficulty, but the people I talked to were uncooperative and often hostile. I sent two letters to the address provided for contributors but never received a response. Such secrecy is understandable since the publishers know that the magazine's pornographic content could cause the police to impound the press at any time.
3 I believe that these stories are not written by the magazine staff for several reasons. Articles usually appeared to be first drafts and conveyed exceedingly raw emotions. In addition, I could not see a reason why the staff would try to degrade their target readership in these stories, especially since they could have provided vivid sexual content in stories about FTZ workers being cheated by men.
4 The term innocent (*ahinsaka*), when used in the context of male-female relationships, means a naive person devoid of sexual knowledge.
5 A worker had clipped the story from an issue of *Priyadari*. Unfortunately, it did not contain a date and the woman merely remembered that it was from an issue published that same year (2000).

6 *Priyadari* 03/05/2003 (vol. 6, no. 31).
7 *Priyadari* 01/28/2000 (vol. 3, no. 26).
8 He uses the term *deiya* twice to address her. This is an unusual honorific for a wife, especially because it refers to god in the masculine form.
9 When this story was read at Disna's boarding house all the women present thought that the young woman faked ignorance regarding sexual matters, because it is considered a male fantasy, to earn the husband's respect and admiration.
10 *Priyadary* 01/08/2005(vol. 8).
11 The magazine publishes readers' responses to these stories. Readers write short letters addressing a particular author to express their interest and asking to get in touch. Women also respond to men's (especially soldiers') sad stories.
12 *Priyadari* 01/21/2004 (vol. 7, no. 24: 13).
13 In a way this reading community was part of an extended network that read and responded to stories. Sometimes women wrote back about the responses they received, and new relationships were forged. In one such case a woman wrote about responses to her story published in the "Scattered Flower Petals" section. In a letter titled "To the Man Who Raped Me" she first thanked the magazine stating that she received letters from all regions of the country ["letters flowed" (*gala awa*)] and that most were from men in the military and the police force offering to make her happy. Then she revealed that the villain in the story had also written to her. Since the story was published he had sent nine letters to Lebanon, where she was working as a house maid. Her letter asked him to compensate for the pain he caused her by never writing to her. See *Priyadari* 01/21/2004 (vol. 7, no. 24: 1, 5).
14 *Priyadari* 03/12/2003 (no. 32: 11).
15 https://freedomhouse.org/report/freedom-net/2013/sri-lanka
16 Sujeewa is also a prolific novelist whose romances are quite popular among Sri Lankan youth. They promote being a good Buddhist, sacrifice, nurturance, sensitivity, innocence, protection, close connections with the temple, and social rituals. In his stories most young men move to the important Buddhist holy city of Anuradhapura to ride out the opposition from the girlfriend's family. There they start commercial enterprises rooted in Buddhist philosophy, ranging from organic farms, flower nurseries, and food courts that do not serve alcohol or meat and prosper until the parents' objections disappear.

References

Bourdieu, P. (1984) *Distinction: A Social Critique of the Judgement of Taste*, trans. by Richard Nice. London: Routledge.
Luff, D. (2001) The Down Right Torture of Women: Moral Lobby Women, Feminists and Pornography. *The Sociological Review.* 49 (1). pp. 78–99.
Modleski, T. (1982) *Loving With a Vengeance: Mass Produced Fantasies for Women.* Connecticut: Archon Books.
Nead, L. (1993) Above the Pulpline: The Cultural Significance of Erotic Art. In Gibson, P. and Gibson, R. (eds.). *Dirty Looks: Women, Pornography, Power.* London: BFI. pp. 144–155.
Radway, J. (1984) *Reading the Romance: Women, Patriarchy and Popular Literature.* Chapel Hill: The University of North Carolina Press.
Segal, L. (1993) Does Pornography Cause Violence?: The Search for Evidence. In Gibson, P. and Gibson, R. (eds.). *Dirty Looks: Women, Pornography, Power.* London: British Film Institute. pp. 5–21.

5 In the service of the nation

Sex, marriage, and social mobility in times of war

Sri Lanka saw a devastating 26-year civil war end in May 2009. The war severely impacted Sri Lankan society, with intense militarization being among its most visible outcomes. In addition to increased numbers of military personnel almost everywhere, this also led to state-sponsored discourses that promoted military men as war heroes and protectors of the nation who were to be appreciated, respected, and loved. Patriotic songs, videos, visuals, and objects, including toys, inundated everyday public and private life, making discussions about war heroes and the war "normal." How did this everyday reality impact FTZ workers, especially in their struggles for sexual agency, well-being, and social mobility? This chapter focuses on how nationalism, militarization, and class-based interests intersected to complicate women workers' struggle for sexual agency and conjugal happiness. It is based on a study of romantic relationships between soldiers and FTZ workers during 2006–2009, when the nationalist/militarist discourses were at their most intense, and during the post war period covering May 2009 to August 2015. The chapter delineates how such relationships engendered conflicts surrounding class status and gender norms and resulted in emotional and physical abuse against workers.

In 2000 the Sri Lankan government declared every June 7th to be War Heroes' Day and said that the very first War Heroes' Day will be celebrated with pomp and pageantry. The celebration included a nationwide two-minute silence observed at 9:00 a.m. to honor all fallen and currently serving soldiers fighting the separatist militants in the Northern and Eastern Provinces. For a few days, female workers at the Suishin FTZ garment factory sought permission from Sanuja, the Floor Coordinator, to observe the two-minute silence in honor of their brothers and boyfriends in the armed forces. Although Sanuja flatly refused the request, on the designated day at 9:00 a.m. many women stopped work and stood up in silence. In a bid to save face, Sanuja hurried to the middle of the shop floor and announced that the factory was observing the moment of silence and that everybody should stand up. The workers spent about five minutes paying respects while some wiped away tears in memory of their loved ones on the battle field.

Considering the emphasis on target production and the resultant strict discipline regarding work schedules in FTZ garment factories, this was indeed a victory for workers. Senior workers belonging to different assembly lines had secretly planned this action during their lunch breaks. Since it was usually difficult to get all workers together to organize even a pleasure trip, the popular support this act garnered surprised many factory officials. Workers obviously shared a sense of loyalty toward their brothers and boyfriends in the armed forces. But how did loyalty to military personnel become a rallying point for oppressed women workers toiling at a transnational factory?

Our heroes in the field

In 2000, as the civil war between the armed forces and separatist LTTE kept raging in the Northern and Eastern Provinces and the number of dead climbed, government propaganda targeted the predominantly Sinhala Buddhist South seeking recruits to the military's lower ranks. Government and privately owned media establishments increasingly portrayed soldiers as heroes who protected the nation (as symbolized by the Sinhala Buddhists). The word *ranawiruwa* (war hero) was rapidly incorporated into everyday conversation as standard identification for all those in the military. There were songs, poems, and novels written about the heroism of military personnel. Several films depicted soldiers' nobility and sacrifices, either as the main or sub-theme. Newspapers and weekly magazines through poetry and short stories and television via teledramas joined forces to remind their readers/viewers daily that soldiers' young lives were being sacrificed to protect the country's sovereignty and that they deserved respect, honor, and love from all patriotic citizens. Schools, temples, and charity organizations conducted ceremonies to fete local *ranawiruwan* and their parents, and military motifs were increasingly displayed on tee shirts, hats, coffee mugs, greeting cards, bumper stickers, and toys.

The militarization of society began in the 1980s and intensified in the 1990s so that by 2006 the Strategic Foresight Group branded Sri Lanka the most militarized state in South Asia (2006: 12). According to Cynthia Enloe, people are militarized once they become fascinated with the military, weapons, and war and begin to consider this to be natural and unproblematic (2000: 2). Militaristic ideologies thus sneak into ordinary routines and people become militarized in their thinking and in the way they make decisions daily (2000: 2).

In Sri Lanka, too, such militarized thinking eventually manifested in gendered terms, resulting in expectations that women show extra concern for soldiers and keep them comfortable when on leave. In reality, these women comfort providers also included sex workers who flocked to the cities that held transition camps for soldiers. But married and unmarried women who had lower ranking military personnel as partners and middle class women married to high ranking military officers were considered the more "honorable" unpaid welfare providers to the nation's protectors. Militarization resulted not only in valorizing patriotic mothering but also in the subtle understanding that women in soldiers' lives should comfort them in class-specific ways.

Caught in between broader nationalist expectations of ideal womanly behavior and contemporary demands (conveyed much more subtly) on women's services to war heroes, workers' romances often ended up in abortions and attempted suicides. However, the workers' expressed loyalty to patriotic ideals and gendered national duties also evidenced tactics through which they reconciled contradictory realities: maintaining innocent "good woman" reputations and ensuring they enjoyed romances and possible married life with men who could potentially provide for a better life than average village men. The particular ways in which these men and women got used (only to be thereafter discarded) within transnational production and the war affected their social status and respectability in different ways, thus leading to a mutual, yet asymmetrical, exploitative relationship between those in the two groups.

Many writings explicate how over time wars and resultant cultures of violence produce new social formations in relation to which people re-fashion their lives (Utas 2005; Winslow and Woost 2005; Thiranagama 2013). Sri Lanka's protracted conflict had produced a war time economy that created thousands of new jobs even as it led to an annual military budget that approximated a billion dollars in the early 2000s (Chaitanya 2006: 11–41). While poor, unemployed males found the military a good source of employment, others generated income by providing auxiliary services to the military, leading to certain political and business leaders making huge commissions from weapons contracts. Just as elite and marginalized sections of society differently adjust their lives in relation to the war, men and women strategize their existence as best benefits them under the constraints and opportunities presented by the war. Factory workers, as a group of women positioned at multiple layers of marginalization, were among those who made complex decisions as an economy dominated by transnational production and war provided them both challenges and opportunities.

Catherine Lutz (2002) draws our attention to groups of people who are "friendly fire casualties of war," such as impoverished people living around U.S. military communities, women who leave their home towns to escape objectification after the military has moved in, and women who daily suffer violence at the hands of their men who live near military posts where violence and male privilege are a "stock in trade" (288). Similarly, I investigate spaces that usually do not get analyzed within the context of militarized violence (or any sort of violence) and try to show how gendered working class groups are differently affected by social status and gender norm ambiguities generated by the political economic demands of a country experiencing rapid trade liberalization and effects of civil war.

Though couched within the vocabulary of patriotic duty, workers' fascination with military men was also rooted in economic rationalizing in that workers found soldiers to be better suitors with stable incomes and more social prestige when compared to other lower class men such as three-wheeler drivers, payment hawkers, and male industrial workers who also competed for workers' attention. While military service was dangerous and could portend early widowhood, women still found soldiers an attractive marriage option since the government paid war widows substantial compensation in addition to soldiers' salaries and pensions. The relationships with soldiers more often than not included sexual activities that clashed with taboos on premarital sex and nationalist ideals of women's purity.

The girlfriends and other women at the boarding houses responded to these conflicting demands via a narratively constructed dichotomy that differentiated between noble (military) men and weak (civilian) men.

By couching their relationships within the rubric of national duty, the women ensured that they were in a position to salvage some respectability should things turn sour. For example, when relationships ended in unwanted pregnancies many women workers claimed that they had premarital sex only because they did not have the heart to say "no" to a war hero. Some women also manipulated the tolerance associated with military relationships to their advantage. For example, Gayani found that she was pregnant with her civilian boyfriend's baby and soon realized the man was avoiding her. She moved to a new boarding house and told everyone that the child's father was killed in the war while they were waiting to be married when he was next on vacation. Residents and the boarding house owner rallied around her and helped her to get an abortion and rebuild her life. In this context whether a woman is a victim of friendly fire or an agent is case-specific. What is clear is the complex and contradictory ways in which patriotism and economic rationalizing coalesce when women make decisions about romantic relationships and sex with military men.

Military work

While there still remain substantial numbers of unemployed and under-employed rural youth, the pressures stemming from intense rural unemployment had some-what eased in the South during the 1990s. One reason for this was FTZs providing assembly line work for rural young women in garment factories. The other was the way the civil war increased demand for soldiers. Consequently, some young men began sarcastically saying, "It is garments for girls and the military for boys."

While rural young men usually joined the armed forces at the lowest rank, during war their labor was highly valued and, therefore, well compensated. As government employees, they were/are paid a comparatively good salary and provided free medical care. In time of war their salary was increased through many additional payments, such as risk area allowance, housing allowance, and payments for forgone leave. There were other ancillary benefits inspired by ongoing discourses, which constructed soldiers as the nation's noble saviors. These included priority in school admissions for military men's children, priority at doctor's offices, post offices, and even at the butcher shop and fish market.[1] They were invited as honorary guests at local temples, schools, and community activities and generally held in high regard by all. As the death toll mounted each day, the colorful portrayal of heroism displayed by soldiers in media discourses intensified and people, especially women, showered them with much love and affection when they returned from the war zone on vacation. For instance, one popular song that was frequently aired during 1999–2000 claimed that "The soldiers are like a golden gate that protects the country from enemies and that all Sri Lankan mothers' breasts are full of milk for them." The *Priyadari* magazine printed a standard weekly blessing on the front page directly below its masthead saying: "This is our respect and blessings for you, who took arms to protect the country."[2] This militarized culture ensured a steady stream of willing recruits from rural areas, even as they were called sacrificial lambs in counter discourses.

Sri Lanka's armed forces – comprising Army, Navy, Air Force, Special Task Force, and Home Guards – at the end of the war numbered over 300,000. Until the mid-1980s, military service represented a respectable career with little danger and the opportunity for socio-economic upward mobility. The civil war, however, brought about a sudden need for more personnel, and it led the government to drastically alter qualifying standards to lure men especially into the lower ranks. This in turn meant that youth from rural and marginalized families were now able to enter government service as soldiers. Sri Lanka's military hierarchy closely corresponds to the existing class hierarchy, with men from rural and poor families dominating the lower ranks while the officer corps hail from middle class families (DeVotta 2007: 21). It is common to hear of officers using abusive language and sometimes even physically abusing the lower ranks to supposedly discipline them. All of this, combined with the constant fear of terrorist attacks, made soldiers' service stressful.

Same social class, different social constructions

While the government and the military considered lower ranking military personnel as expendable human resources, the inflated war hero image provided soldiers an opportunity for social mobility. For example, in 2007 the Sri Lanka Navy launched a recruitment campaign using scenarios familiar to rural people. The ads did not ask the young men to enlist because it was their national duty to do so; instead, they depicted how sailors enjoyed greater demand within the marriage market.

Television advertisement 1

Two elderly women holding flower trays walk down the temple stairs, discussing their respective families. They appear not to have seen each other in a while.

WOMAN 1: That son who went to Peradeniya [university] – what does he do?
WOMAN 2: He is [working] in the bank.
WOMAN 1: And the daughter?
WOMAN 2: She is a teacher.
WOMAN 1 (in a sympathetic tone): Only the youngest son . . . [suggesting he is a problem].
WOMAN 2 (with annoyance at the question and obvious pride): He is in the Navy.
Flash of the Navy seal, and a voice stating, "Sri Lanka Navy – a university in the middle of the ocean."
WOMAN 1 (with lot of interest in her voice): My youngest daughter is very well educated. The age is good too [suggesting the two would make a good match]
WOMAN 2 (with an arrogant tilt of her head): I'll think about it.
The ad ends with the sailor's mother walking past the other woman.

Television advertisement 2

A matchmaker is visiting the mansion of an aristocrat. The latter shows him no respect or hospitality.

MATCHMAKER: The prospective groom's brother is an engineer. His sister is an English teacher.
ARISTOCRAT (with no enthusiasm): Ok, ok, what does the prospective groom do?
MATCHMAKER: He is in the Navy.
Flash of the Navy seal, and a narrator states, "Sri Lankan Navy – the university in the middle of the ocean."
ARISTOCRAT (appearing to get up with a big smile): Matchmaker sit, sit. Daughter, (who seems to be in a different section of the house) bring this matchmaker uncle a cup of tea.

These ads were remarkable in the way they sought to equate Navy service with a highly prestigious position in Sri Lankan society: being a graduate of one of the handful of universities.

Another government jingle, titled "*We Are For Us*," depicted soldiers in family environments – paying respects to elders, helping children, and getting married in lavish military style ceremonies – while a background singer crooned, "This child has thousand mothers, and he is a blood relative of the whole nation. . . ." The advertisement used male and female models and middle class symbols, further fueling FTZ workers' hopes that military men were a ladder to achieving modernity. Furthermore, military training, discipline, and sub-cultural attitudes and styles initiated changes in soldiers' cognitive dispositions, which also created the possibility of envisioning class mobility. While military culture has helped portray soldiers as a "privileged group," the social stigma associated with the FTZ has caused soldiers to consider FTZ workers a convenient source for temporary pleasure who are nevertheless unsuitable for marriage.

Most soldiers are also from villages but by virtue of their employment they can aspire to building homes near regional capitals or in villages with more facilities and better transportation. Desiring to stay in urban areas and attain at least some symbols of modernity, women willingly started relationships with such men who promised them lives away from the drudgery of their native villages. But most of the time these relationships ended in misery, and this was related to their image as women who transgressed ideal norms of behavior and the resultant stigma. Intense anxieties about mobile women's morality created an image of FTZ workers as women with loose virtues who could be easily deceived into having sexual relationships. The soldiers who gravitated toward Katunayake in their free time or on weekends looking for girlfriends were no different from the other men who did likewise.

As members of rural, marginalized families themselves, workers had brothers, cousins, neighbors, and former school friends serving in war torn areas. Through these relatives and friends, the workers befriended soldiers and got into relationships. In 2000, when the so-called third phase of the civil war between the government and the LTTE was at its peak, many workers I met at Suishin and at the boarding house I stayed at had boyfriends in the armed forces. The conversations at the factory and boarding houses (to varying degrees) centered on their loved ones at the war front. The workers went in groups to the nearby temple to conduct *bodhi pujas*[3] or to famous shrines or ritual specialists seeking to ensure the safe return of these soldiers.

As rural Sri Lankan women, FTZ workers earnestly desired marriage and sincerely believed that their relationships with soldiers would end up in marriage. Although they firmly held that their boyfriends were not bad men, workers knew that these relationships could result in misery and even tragedy. There were stories of soldiers who would befriend a worker, promise her marriage, have sexual relations and thereafter vanish without a trace. There were soldiers who had relationships with two or three FTZ workers at the same time without the women having any clue as to the others' existence. There were soldiers who also had relationships with FTZ workers while their wives lived in villages. Occasionally one heard of soldiers getting married to their global worker girlfriends. But one mostly heard of FTZ workers getting cheated, abused, and abandoned by military men. This evidenced that the soldiers considered FTZ workers a pool of women from which they could find partners to fulfill their short term sexual needs. This is perhaps a good place to recall the last chapter, which included accounts from *Priyadari* that discussed how military boyfriends were cheated and mistreated by FTZ workers. Given the large number of women in the FTZ, there surely must have been some FTZ workers who did not care much about war heroes' feelings, but most relationships involving military men seemed to follow the familiar pattern of soldiers cheating and mistreating FTZ workers.

Romances, sex, and national duty

As noted earlier, many FTZ workers had relatives and friends in the armed forces and these servicemen befriended other women workers whenever they came to visit. As the country's major airport was located close to the FTZ, a permanent Air Force camp located just outside the airport maintained several check-points throughout the area surrounding the airport and FTZ. In addition, there was a military transit camp that was located in Seeduwa in close proximity to workers' boarding houses. Consequently, the area was characterized, especially before the end of the war, by the presence of both large numbers of young, unmarried women and soldiers who were in romantic relationships.

Once when staying at Saman's boarding house I, together with some other workers, counted the residents and collected information on their military connections.[4] All the residents present that night claimed they had brothers or cousins at the war front. Sixteen workers had boyfriends in the armed forces or police. Eight workers confessed to having had relationships with military men that had turned sour. The women who did not currently have boyfriends preferred to start a relationship with a member of the armed forces. The eight women who had non-military boyfriends gave various reasons – the danger of the profession and military men not having much time for families – as to why they preferred other men. Four confided that they would most probably have started a relationship with a soldier had they met one before getting into their current relationships.

When discussing her relationship with an army soldier, Devika pointed out that "It is due to a good deed I have done in my previous birth that I now have the opportunity to make a war-hero, who is protecting the country and the nation, happy." In fact, many women who had military boyfriends were given to such rhetoric and their impassioned speeches in such instances closely resembled the media glossing on stories of military wives and families. Most weekly papers and magazines carried stories of long suffering women waiting patiently for their husbands, sons, and brothers to come home from the war front. They also carried poems, short stories and serialized cartoons that valorized these women as contemporary heroines who sacrificed as much for the nation as did soldiers. Television dramas, films, and songs also contributed to creating an image of a "good woman" who served the nation by caring and comforting their military men-folk and preserving their honor by consciously disciplining their movements while they were away at the battlefield. *Priyadari* and *Suwanda* also carried such stories, and women often used the same passionate nationalistic language when expressing love and loyalty to military boyfriends. Workers' relationships with military men were aided and admired not only by other workers, boarding house owners, and factory officials but also by wider society, which usually looked down on FTZ workers. The special attention they received was evident at the boarding houses when soldiers visited their girlfriends on bi-monthly vacations. When one arrived everyone made it a point to greet him and ask after his health and comforts. Meanwhile, most workers helped the girlfriend cook a nice meal for the soldier. I even saw women volunteering to wash soldiers' clothes.

The general rule at the boarding house was that visiting boyfriends should sleep in the main house with Saman instead of spending the night in boarding rooms. However, when soldier boyfriends visited, the other occupants tried to give him some privacy with his girlfriend. In one such incident a soldier boyfriend visited his girlfriend, who was one of my roommates, after three months. The other occupants, including myself, decided to get out of the room and sleep on the verandah. Although it was cold and the floor was uneven, we all soon fell asleep. But around 12:30 in the morning the soldier came out of the room saying, "Up, up, little sisters, go inside." His tone did not leave much space for protest and gathering our sleeping mats and pillows we went inside the room. His girlfriend, busily ironing his clothes, explained how she had spent all this time listening to his stories about the battlefield. Despite the sounds of love making we heard through the thin walls, she almost convinced us that all she did was to simply fulfill her national duty by providing a sympathetic ear to her war hero. Using language commonly used in mass media representations of war, she thus reconciled the broader nationalistic expectations of her premarital purity with the everyday demands on working class females to execute their national duty by providing comforting services to lower ranked military men. It is the need to reconcile these contradictory expectations that more often than not lead FTZ workers into difficult circumstances. In the following section I discuss the forms of violence that typically ensued within these military romances.

Everyday violence within romantic relationships

The way militarization increases violence against women has received much attention (Vigil 2014; Staudt and Mendez 2015). Yasmin Tamibiah has explored how sexualities in Sri Lanka are constructed and controlled in the interests of militarized, nationalist projects, especially with regard to sex workers and female militants (2004, 2005). Irrespective of whether they are relatives of soldiers, militants, sex workers, or internally displaced people, women face serious violence in war-torn societies (De Mel 2001, 2015; Giles and Hyndman 2004; Tambiah 2004, 2005; Wijayatilake 2004; Coulter 2009; Hewamanne 2010, 2015). Despite the substantial body of work on militarization and violence, everyday violence that occurs within legally or socially sanctioned relationships has not received much attention. This is especially true for violence committed within sanctioned domestic spaces such as marriages and relationships. Studying the effects of militarized nationalist projects on intimate spaces, and their consequences on reproducing the same militarized culture, is vital for a comprehensive portrayal of war and war-time social formations. Pradeep Jeganathan terms the maneuvering of numerous military check points in Colombo as "walking through violence" and points toward many ways in which war-related violence seeps into everyday life even in non-combat areas (2002). Similarly, militarization processes interacted with specific socio-economic conditions in complex ways to produce consent among women to undergo and tolerate subtle and not so subtle forms of violence by military men within their romantic relationships.

Usually, FTZ workers criticized boyfriends who were abusive and spoke disparagingly of girlfriends who stuck with such men. In fact, several women confided that they ended relationships after experiencing abusive behavior. Yet, these same workers reacted differently to similar forms of violence when committed by military men as opposed to civilian boyfriends. Influenced by the war-time media construction of the soldier as a larger than life persona, girlfriends and other FTZ women excused and forgave *ranawiru* boyfriends for behavior that they normally found reprehensible.

The military boyfriends usually tried to portray a calm, patient, tolerant, and paternalistic attitude in their association with other residents in the boarding house. They called all the women, including myself, "*nangi,*" (younger sister) and showed concern for everyone's wellbeing. They contributed generously if there was a collection being made for a trip or a donation toward a worker's family. During festival times they volunteered to take groups of women out to see decorations, musical shows, or movies. Most of them were infectiously jovial and teased and solicited women and lambasted men who mistreated women.

In fact, I have never seen a military boyfriend physically abusing a woman in public. But some women occasionally confided how they heard about some women getting beaten by their military boyfriends inside their rooms. In most such cases they attempted to justify this by claiming that some misdeed provoked the beatings. While they agreed it was not the right way to respond, they always ended up providing excuses for the soldier. They emphasized how stressful and anxiety ridden the war zone was and held that girlfriends of military men should be extra careful about the feelings and moods of their boyfriends. In one *Priyadari* story, a garment factory worker noted how military girlfriends should not be too sentimental and demand attention from their boyfriends. Instead she suggested that they should be able to face any challenge and be disciplined when dealing with the outside world.[5] Another *Priyadari* article, written by a military wife, was titled, "Soldiers' Wives Should Be Able to Tolerate and Sacrifice a Lot."[6]

These justifications aside, it was obvious that workers were very conflicted about how to respond to these overt acts of physical abuse. Within everyday conversations they struggled to find a balance between their loyalties to war hero loved ones and the growing awareness of their rights as women and human beings. Even when writing to *Priyadari* about military boyfriends mistreating them, women were cautious to differentiate between war heroes and occasional abusers. In one such story a FTZ worker wrote, "The military has such honest boys and I always loved military men . . . it was my rotten luck that I found this animal who destroyed me."[7] In addition to differentiating abusers as the few who shamed the heroes, they simultaneously emphasized the highly stressful character of the battlefield. They had greater trouble, however, in recognizing violence against women when such actions manifested in subtler forms in the behavioral, emotional, and psychological realms.

Most of the soldiers seemed preoccupied with the effect on their honor if women misbehaved in any way. While girlfriends usually participated in FTZ fashions and displayed newly acquired poise, when soldiers came to visit most took on a timid, quiet demeanor in contrast to their usual boisterous, jovial manner. However, the subtle everyday violence was mostly manifested through these men's callous attitude toward their girlfriends. Although workers liked military men for their national service and similarities in class background, the men seemed to consider themselves better than FTZ workers. When I talked to several soldiers attached to the Vauniya Army Camp in 2003, they said they preferred to marry innocent (ignorant of sexual knowledge), sheltered young women who have never migrated to urban areas or the Middle East as domestics. When I asked how it was that most military men have FTZ girlfriends, a couple said that FTZ workers are for fun and not for marriage. They were very expressive about their preferences for marriage partners and why they would not consider FTZ workers good prospects. The commonly given answer was that most FTZ workers were corrupted due to their urban life at the FTZ and had ceased to be innocent, respectable women. A soldier who had a FTZ girlfriend at the time said he was not sure whether he would marry her.

His mother was bringing proposals from respected families whose daughters either held more respectable jobs (teachers, clerks, nurses) or had dowry, and he thought he most probably would end up marrying one of those women.

When my research associate interviewed several other soldiers in Batticoloa in 2005 and 2012, he received similar answers. The soldiers he talked to also recounted stories about other soldiers who used and abused FTZ girlfriends while their wives waited for them in the village and expressed conflictual feelings about this behavior. They tried to justify their fellow soldiers' behavior by noting that it was a woman's responsibility to protect her purity. Several, however, also noted that it is a sin to take advantage of women and abandon them. Most soldiers we talked to had sisters and cousins working in the FTZ, but still said they would try to marry up rather than marrying a FTZ worker. One soldier, Ranjith, noted that he wished his FTZ worker sister would never fall for a soldier as he knew first-hand how soldiers looked down upon FTZ workers who were not relatives.

This attitude manifested itself in the way some military men treated FTZ workers. During my stay at the boarding house two women found out that the soldiers they had been dating were in fact married. Ajitha came across her military man arm in arm with another FTZ worker. Together the two women found out that he, in fact, had a third girlfriend working in yet another FTZ factory. In less than two months after breaking up with this military man, Ajitha started a relationship with another soldier and by the time I left was making *bodhi pujas* to ensure the safe return of her new boyfriend from the war zone.

Janaki was another resident at Saman's boarding house who was in a relationship with a soldier. During the first six months Janaki saw this man only twice and they only talked. This non-interest in physical intimacy made Janaki gush about his good morals and how lucky she was to have him as a boyfriend. But the third time he visited her he asked her to accompany him to his village as his mother was very ill and needed help. Janaki came running to the room the rest of us were in asking what she should do. Taking women out on long journeys on phony reasons is a ploy boyfriends, both military men and civilians, seeking sexual pleasure often resort to. We reminded Janaki that this could be such a trap and she should not go anywhere unless their marriage was registered. When Janaki related this, the man erupted into a violent outburst and tore her photographs saying he would find a woman who satisfied his needs. Janaki was inconsolable for about a week, and her friends tried to comfort her by saying that she was better off without such a man who put other war heroes to shame. Janaki later tried to contact the man and found out that the telephone number he had provided was not a working number. Her letters also went unanswered, which finally convinced her to give up hope. Several other workers also found that the phone numbers and addresses given them were of no use when they tried to find a particular soldier who had vanished after having sexual relationships. While all sorts of men who frequented the FTZ resorted to such tactics, the particular positioning of soldiers as war heroes made women more vulnerable to being pressured for sex.

Military men's non-FTZ worker girlfriends mostly lived with their parents or were boarded at women's hostels overseen by educational institutions. Due to the internalized ideas of what a good Sinhala woman is, soldiers usually had more respect for women who lived under family authority. Several FTZ workers and soldiers claimed that some soldiers have a girlfriend or two at the FTZ while maintaining stable, family sanctioned relationships with women deemed more respectable and eventually married the latter. While there were soldiers who truly cared for their FTZ girlfriends and later married them, many others were clearly in such relationships for temporary fun.

I discussed with a senior military officer the way married soldiers deceived women and then abandoned them. He opined that if women were stupid enough to be deceived he did not see much wrong in soldiers taking sexual advantage of them. "These are men who do not get to see Sinhala women for months at a time, and how can one begrudge them for trying to have some pleasure. It is the women who should know how to protect their purity," he said. As I noted earlier, senior military men seemed to privately concur that soldiers and FTZ workers, being from marginalized sections of society, are bound to be attracted to each other, and if women were brazen enough to challenge dominant cultural values and find boyfriends they deserved the subsequent callous treatment.

Performance of innocence

Soldiers' girlfriends and wives wrote to *Priyadari* about how their men were eager for sexual relations when they visited on vacation and how they spent most of the vacation enjoying different sexual activities. The authors sounded sympathetic of even unfair sexual demands and wrote how they complied because of the soldiers' service to the nation. For example, one author wrote how she had to have sex on a day she was having her period as her military partner came home and could not wait to have sex.[8] Whether written by real life military partners or the magazine editor, reading such stories weekly intensified women's notions of obligation to war heroes and shaped their responses to military men's advances.

The relentless social pressure to be good and understanding toward war heroes, and their developing consciousness as industrial workers more often than not led FTZ girlfriends to respond in contradictory ways to specific situations. Living in an urban space FTZ workers developed new tastes and acquired new knowledges that were kept secret from unmarried women. However, the men they befriended were socialized into ideal norms of gendered behavior and more or less expected their girlfriends to be as close to the ideal as possible. As a result, workers attempted to create an image of themselves as women who continued to value rural customs.

Sri Lankan women generally expected their relationships to end in marriage. FTZ workers described their boyfriends as "the man I am going to marry." If the men abandoned them after some time, their reputations were tarnished and their parents found it difficult to arrange a good marriage. This made many FTZ workers hang on to the relationships by any means, including having sexual intercourse even when they did not desire such intimacy. Women who had boyfriends and feared the men would pressure them into having intercourse still tried to come across as "innocent young women" who lacked any understanding of how sexual advances and activities unfolded.

The performance of innocence required women to disavow knowledge of contraceptives, leading to unwanted pregnancies. While inaccessibility of contraceptives complicated the situation, women were more constrained by ideologies that dictated it was shameful for unmarried women to start using contraceptives. This fear is not without cause as young men, influenced by dominant notions of female morality, did in fact regard women who used contraceptives to be akin to prostitutes. In a story in *Priyadari* one soldier explained how he dumped his girlfriend when he found contraceptive pills inside a secret panel in her handbag. He describes his feelings as follows: "I could not believe what I saw. I got disgusted with her."[9]

Their quest to gratify men's fantasies of leading an innocent virgin into sexual activities was what partly lead to unwanted pregnancies and, sometimes, to sexually transmitted diseases. Although cultural values continue to get reconfigured, the reluctance in official discourses and media to abandon moralistic vocabulary confounded workers' attempts to attain long term empowerment through global factory work. These moralist vocabularies force women to pretend and perform at least some aspects of ideal womanhood in spaces where it is impossible to be "ideal." Judging by the stories circulating in boarding houses about the high number of abortions performed on military girlfriends, this dilemma only seems to lead women toward more violence at roadside abortion clinics.

Pregnancies and abortions

On one occasion at Saman's boarding house, a woman laid on the floor of her room moaning loudly. Nilanthi attended to Kamani's needs and came back with news that we all suspected and feared: Kamani had gone through another abortion, this being the third since she started working at the FTZ. For days many of us discussed the situation regarding abortions in low voices. We shared what we each knew of illegal abortion clinics around the area, their abysmal conditions and the stories we had heard of operations ending fatally. One topic discussed was why it was mostly military girlfriends who were rumored to have gone through abortions. Women discussed how it must be hard to say no to a man who fought against the national enemy in jungles for months on end. As Nadee said, "When considering how even weak men cannot let their girlfriends alone, one can understand how army folk feel when they see their girlfriends after so many months." This statement closely resembled the view of the army officer I described earlier. The women too focused not on the worker desiring sexual intercourse, but on the relief of seeing the man alive again and the desire to make him happy. As Shyamala said, "I do not want to stop hugging him when I see him after two months. I cling onto him until he gets embarrassed and pushes me away." As noted earlier, women did not talk about desire directly but alluded to it through culturally acceptable terms, and it is possible that they themselves may not be fully aware of their feelings.

Unwanted pregnancies often ended in violent forms of termination at roadside abortion clinics around the FTZ area (Hettiarachchy and Schensul 2001; Hewamanne 2010). Abortion is illegal in Sri Lanka, except when performed to save the life of the mother.[10] However, the Executive Director of the Family Planning Association of Sri Lanka (FPASL) holds that about 400 backstreet abortions per day are being carried out in the country.[11] According to reports from doctors, midwives, and NGO staff members, the number of illegal abortions per year in Katunayake seems very high.

As already noted, many boyfriends discarded their girlfriends once they got pregnant. Accounts of abandonment indicated that the men felt they fulfilled their duty when they provided the cost of an abortion. Although I managed to visit two small abortion clinics in the area, I was not able to learn much about the medical procedures other than that both places used an injection that would induce abortion. Several three-wheeler taxi drivers who transported me back and forth from these centers noted that there were places that used poisonous herbs (*endaru kiri*) to abort the fetus, and that in some places women were first sexually abused by the abortion performer and his friends. Although the violence at roadside clinics results from a multitude of causes, including government hypocrisy about the reproductive needs of young people, the pressures on military girlfriends to provide comforting services to war heroes during war time exacerbate the risk factors for women workers.

Rationalizing within romances

According to Berdhal and Malone, economic motives and commercial agendas during wars is not a new phenomenon (2000: 1). Mats Utas notes how women can exercise forms of agency while socially navigating war zones. According to Utas, young females in the Liberian Civil War were active agents who alternatively used different tactics – becoming girlfriends of military officers, enrolling as soldiers themselves, or prostituting – to maintain social networks, cope with challenges, and to exploit the opportunities presented by the civil war (2005: 406). While the civil war's effects on Sri Lanka's global workers was very different from what Liberian women experienced, the workers' seemingly blind reverence for soldiers within asymmetrical and risky relationships is not mere adherence to discourses on gendered duties to the nation or a simple effect of the militarization of society. Instead, it is a complex combination of factors that also mesh with social and economic aspirations and better futures through association with working class men who seem to offer better opportunities. In that sense, the romantic relationships are a step toward claiming a stake in the economy of war and ensuring a secure future when FTZ employment is no more.

The economic and social rationalizing that influence the decision to start a relationship with a military person as opposed to a civilian was not usually expressed directly in daily conversations. Rather, it was conveyed through certain decisions and preferences as well as occasional unintentional utterances. Such utterances showed that economic and other rationalizations are intertwined with their nationalistic admiration of military men. As a result of the better diet in the barracks and daily physical workouts, the men had muscular bodies and boasted better physiques than most other young men around the FTZ area. Influenced by their military training, soldiers, even when on vacation, dressed neatly and were clean shaven. All this made them a cut above their competitors for FTZ workers' attention. Moreover, soldiers took their girlfriends to nicer restaurants and provided them with other entertainment opportunities. Girlfriends also talked about the special attention they received in buses, restaurants and shops when people recognized the men as soldiers.

"Those days when the war was raging, a van from the *Ranawiru Sevene* (the rehabilitation center for disabled soldiers) dropped disabled soldiers around the bazzar and boarding houses every Sunday. These girls are very kind to soldiers. They treat the disabled ones even more generously. It is as if the military was trying to take advantage of this kindness," said Himali, who was in charge of the Women's Counseling Center at Katunayake in July 2005.[12] Following this lead as well as my own observations of their kindness toward disabled military men, I asked several workers, with whom I was traveling to the Kithulgala scenic river area in a hired van, why FTZ workers seemed to like disabled military men. They all claimed that the military men's noble service to the country influenced their concern. But Aruni perhaps best explained why they preferred a disabled soldier over a physically fit civilian man who did not have a good job: "Disabled soldiers get their salary but do not have to go to war. So you don't have to suffer in fear for their lives. They need our help too. So unlike the others, they would appreciate and will marry the girlfriends and would love us more for our sacrifices for them. How meritorious (*pin*) it is to take care of a soldier who has gotten disabled for the country than to be with men to whom we ourselves have to provide for," she said in a matter of fact voice.

Aruni's statement points toward a local logic in which the workers reconcile the realities of their lives by using patriotism and Buddhist ethics while at the same time strategizing the best possible married life for themselves. De Mel notes that disabled soldiers felt that the social capital they acquired as active, able bodied military men was now lost due to their disabilities (2003/04: 122). In such a vulnerable position, disabled soldiers seem to find FTZ worker girlfriends to be worthy of their respect.

In 2000 and again in 2008, I observed that most workers went on revering men who deserted the army and were in hiding from the military police.[13] Sujani began a relationship with a soldier and thereafter took up popular rhetoric of women's duty toward them. But a few weeks later when she heard that he had deserted his army post, she nonchalantly accepted the situation and did all she could to keep his location a secret. Deepthi was also involved with an army deserter who worked at a garment factory to prevent being arrested. When he was caught and remanded to the Seeduwa police station, women at Saman's boarding house went to see him and shed tears. If women's attraction was based on soldiers' financial solvency, desertion, which stripped the soldiers of their salary, should cause women to act less reverently.

Desertion, however, occurred in a particular cultural context that both soldiers and the workers shared. The military was in dire need of personnel during the war and was forced to compromise its disciplinary standards. Lower ranked military men had learned to manipulate this war time need to their advantage. According to several military officers I spoke to, soldiers would work for about four months to collect enough money and then desert the army post to enjoy the money. When they ran out of money they returned to the headquarters, went through the mandatory cell-time, and started military service again. According to an officer, some soldiers had done this over and over again.

Describing what she thought of her boyfriend deserting the army, Sujani said "Oh, it is just for a short time. He will go back when the paddy-work season ends." In fact, it turned out that many soldiers deserted their posts between the months of June–August when the north-eastern monsoon brought rains for dry-zone paddy cultivation. When the season was over, they found a way to go back into military service. Soldiers also confided that many deserted when their parents were ill and they feared that the parents would die before they had a chance to see them again. Hailing from agricultural villages themselves, FTZ workers easily understood the logic of this pattern and held onto their boyfriends with the understanding that they would return to duty when the time was right. These situations showed that there are complex social, economic, and cultural reasons for FTZ workers' attraction to military men.

Post civil war, global workers, and soldiers

In May 2009 government forces ended the civil war and also killed LTTE leader Vellupillai Prabakaran. On 18 May, the government declared the war won, and wild celebrations broke out in majority Sinhala areas. These celebrations further inflated the war hero image and led to people paying respect to military families, naming newborn babies after certain prominent military officials, and proposals being made for houses to be built for valiant soldiers.

However, the following months saw a bitter political battle between the army commander, General Sarath Fonseka, and the political leadership. Fonseka, while still in uniform, had made clear he wanted to enter politics, and the government, apparently afraid that the general would acquire a cult following, sought to curtail his powers by forcing him to retire with a ceremonial position. The events leading up to this created much resentment and the main opposition party propped up the retired Fonseka as its presidential candidate. Rajapaksa enjoyed greater momentum and ended up easily defeating Fonseka in the January 2010 presidential election. In an act that was clearly motivated by revenge, President Rajapaksa thereafter had Fonseka dragged out of his office and arrested for supposed "military offenses." He was subsequently court marshalled and spent over two years in prison (DeVotta 2011). Many considered his post-election treatment to be exceedingly humiliating. But his silencing helped the government to shift the focus of valorization away from the military toward political leaders.

My interviews with workers and their families in October 2009 showed that many still viewed military men as larger-than-life war heroes who deserved more love and respect than others. Such sentiments suggest that power relations engendered by the intersections of the political economy of war and transnational production may continue in some form, although by 2012 many soldiers were already airing doubts about the extent of the nation's gratitude toward them.

This may have been partly inspired by government propaganda promoting a certain notion of ethnic and religious unity. The constant barrage of songs and military images between TV programs had tapered off, and although there were many special features on the war, the valorization of soldiers was no longer common on TV. In addition, in an effort to manage the budget, the military had forced retirement on some officers and discharged some voluntary servicemen. It certainly did not help that soldiers were being used post war to farm, sell lunch packets, build schools and bridges, run tea shops and barber salons, and oversee dolphin watching tours. Several soldiers and officers I talked to said they feared their sacrifices would be erased by the state, just as the former army commander had been reduced to a criminal in a jail cell after the war's end. Still, many expressed faith in the general public and thought it would not easily forget the hardships they endured during the war and the sacrifices they made toward ending it. Their families and loved ones worried about this erasure more than the men dared express. Three military wives I spoke to especially worried that the government would discontinue the preferential treatment military men's children were afforded when enrolling in popular public schools. This preferential treatment, however, continued to be in place as of December 2015.

Significant political changes had taken place when I conducted field research in July 2015. Widespread corruption, breakdown in the rule of law, and the rising cost of living had led to President Mahinda Rajapaksa being defeated in the presidential election in January. And Rajapaksa's (failed) attempt to make a political comeback as prime minister through the August parliamentary elections (partly by fanning fears about a possible LTTE revival) was in full swing during my interviews in Katunayake and elsewhere.

It continues to be the case that global factory workers still find military men to be very desirable partners. Military girlfriends and most other workers present at interviews and focus groups pointed to stable salaries, smart attire, and attractive physique and said military men are still a cut above the other men in the area. Unlike during the war, however, they avoided referring to military men as hypermasculine and the other men in the area as weak. Many also had to be prodded to talk about the period when songs, dramas, and videos portrayed soldiers as war heroes, although some felt soldiers deserved special treatment given their service to the country.

When the conversation turned to sexual intercourse, all the workers interviewed (15 formally and about 60 informally) said that there was now no reason for women to feel they had to accommodate soldiers' sexual needs given that the war was over. Not a single woman said her boyfriend sought to use his military service to get her to agree to sexual relations, although they did say that the men expressed their interest in having sex in many ways while noting that this was no different from what all women experienced. They all claimed that their boyfriend being in the military alone was not something that would cause them to engage in sexual relations. As Janumi said, "I don't know why him being a soldier should matter. If I am ready for sex, I am. If I am not, then too bad." Many agreed. It continues to be a sad reality around the FTZ area that woman get pressured into having sex whether they are ready to do so or not. Although it seems that the pressures associated with being good to war heroes had eased, without more concentrated ethnographic research it is difficult to determine whether there are significant changes in the dynamics.

There remain conflicting claims as to the number of abortions around the FTZ area. Many workers and NGO officials said the number continues to be high, while some women and boarding house owners claimed that today's workers are more streetwise and know how to prevent pregnancies. Only a few noted that abortions among military girlfriends were more common. Janumy, again, put it very well: "The more desirable the boyfriend and the more stable the job, the more willing a girl is to take the risk. So I guess that could be the case (that military girlfriends are the ones who get abortions more often). It is not like other big gentlemen with good jobs come around here looking for girlfriends."

Although, in the absence of actual numbers, it was hard to determine such changes, I could clearly see a change in the former veneration with which whole boarding houses treated a visiting soldier. They were still welcomed warmly and treated lovingly. But no overt hero-worshipping was visible. Workers did not engage in long, emotional conversations about the war and their war heroes. Girlfriends did not cry and cling onto military men when they left. Many workers said the pride of a girlfriend now solely came from how financially stable a man was and how well he treated her.

Military men continue to be sought after as desirable spouses by middle class and even elite families in villages. With the war now over, there is now less fear among such families that their daughters would end up being widows. That aside, there is the steady income and pension a family can depend on. My interviews with soldiers on vacation in the villages, however, make clear that they continue to think of FTZ women as less desirable marriage partners. When I mentioned that global factory workers now (2015) bring in a good salary, one soldier noted: "*ane* what is the point of money, when nothing else is good (about them)." The end of the war has led to soldiers being less valorized; but it has not changed soldiers' perceptions about FTZ workers, notwithstanding their increased salaries. Worker–soldier romances will therefore continue to bring heartbreaks, abortions, and even suicide, for women at least for some time to come.

Complicated sexual worlds

Describing how the military employed a variety of means to control both men and women in order to achieve its goals, Cynthia Enloe (1983) writes that "Military elites have been as self-conscious as any factory manager about designing and redesigning sexual divisions of labor" (7). Unfortunately for Sri Lankan FTZ women workers, both the transnational factory managers and military seem to think they are an expendable human resource. While factory managers agree on paying women the lowest possible wages, the military seems to appreciate their work as girlfriends as it keeps soldiers away from sex workers.

Romances between soldiers and workers presented an aspect of their sexual worlds that contained many ambiguities with regard to sexual desire. As usual women talked about being pressured for sex and claimed they did not desire sex. Their accounts reiterated the familiar "persuasion, reluctance, more persuasion and giving in" routines. This made it difficult to clearly delineate whether the sex was coerced or desired. In any case, the relationships and stories of tragedies added to the image of "non-discipline" among the workers. What is clear are the complexities surrounding intimate relationships and sexual lives within the FTZ and how workers make decisions about their future lives even as they carefully negotiate varied demands on their bodies and loyalties by boyfriends, families, neighbors, military, and the nation.

Notes

1 Officers resented the indiscriminate use of the term *runawiruwa* and complained that the term lumped all soldiers as war heroes.
2 *Priyadari* 12/13/2006 (vol. 10, no. 21:1).
3 The Buddhist ritual of bathing and decorating the Bodhi tree (*ficus religiosa*) to invoke blessings on loved ones.
4 This included a very informal head count of women and information they provided about their boyfriends.
5 *Priyadari* 09/12/2001 (vol. 5, no. 7: 5).
6 *Priyadari* 05/30/2001 (vol. 4, no. 44: 24).
7 *Priyadari* 07/18/2001 (vol. 4, no. 5: 3).
8 *Priyadari* 12/05/2001 (vol. 5, no. 19: 11).
9 *Priyadari* 10/24/2001 (vol. 5, no. 13: 24).
10 Penal Code, Section 303.
11 *The Island* 09/25/1999.
12 When I related this to a senior military officer he vehemently denied any such practice. However, he relented that this could have been a private arrangement between the driver of the *Ranawiru Sevene* vehicle and the disabled soldiers.
13 Nearly 58,000 soldiers had deserted the military by early 2007 (DeVotta 2007: 21).

References

Berdahl, M. and Malone, D. (eds.) (2000) *Greed and Grievance: Economic Agendas in Civil Wars*. Boulder: Lynne Rienner.

Chaitanya, K. (2006) Cost of War and Its Impact on the Sri Lankan Economy. In Fernando, L. (ed.). *Sri Lanka's Ethnic Conflict in the Global Context*. Colombo: Faculty of Graduate Studies. pp. 11–41.

Coulter, C. (2009) *Bush Wives and Girl Soldiers: Women's Lives through War and Peace in Sierra Leone*. Ithaca: Cornell University Press.

De Mel, N. (2001) *Women and the Nation's Narrative: Gender and Nationalism in Twentieth Century Sri Lanka*. New Delhi: Kali for Women.

De Mel, N. (2003) Marketing War, Marketing Peace. Paper presented at the Workshop on "Home and the World: Changing Ethnic Identities in Sri Lanka" Colombo, Sri Lanka. June 18.

De Mel, N. (2003/04) Staging Pain: Representation, the Disabled Soldier and the Butterflies Theatre of Sri Lanka. *The Sri Lanka Journal of the Humanities*. 29–30 (1–2). pp. 111–129.

De Mel, N. (2015) Between the War and the Sea: Critical Events, Contiguities and Feminist Work in Sri Lanka. *Interventions*. 9 (2). pp. 238–254.

DeVotta, N. (2007) Strategizing Identities in a Civil War: Polyethnicity and Governance in Batticaloa. Paper presented at the Conference on Dialogue on Democracy and Pluralism in South Asia. New Delhi, India. May 1–2 2007.

DeVotta, N. (2011) Sri Lanka: From Turmoil to Dynasty. *Journal of Democracy*. 22 (2) (April). pp. 130–144.

Enloe, C. (1983) *Does Khaki Become You?: The Militarization of Women's Lives*. Boston: South End Press.

Enloe, C. (2000) *Maneuvers: The International Politics of Militarizing Women's Lives*. Berkeley: University of California Press.

Giles, W. and Hyndman, J. (eds.) (2004) *Sites of Violence: Gender and Conflict Zones*. Berkeley: University of California Press.

N.H.V. Gunaratne, Personal Security of Female Factory Workers in the Environs of Free Trade Zones of Sri Lanka: A Study in the Eweriwatte Grama Niladhari Division in the Katunayake Free Trade Zone, Master of Science Thesis submitted to the University of Sri Jayewardenepura (June 2004).

Hettiarachchy, T. and Schensul, S.L. (2001) The Risks of Pregnancy and the Consequences among Young Unmarried Women Working in a Free Trade Zone in Sri Lanka. *Asia Pacific Population Journal*. 16 (2). pp. 125–140.

Hewamanne, S. (2010) Gendering the Internally Displaced: Problem Bodies, Fluid Boundaries and Politics of Civil Society Participation in Sri Lanka. *International Journal of Women's Studies*. 11 (1). pp. 157–172.

Hewamanne, S. (2015) Complicated Belonging: Gendered Empowerment and Anxieties about 'Returning' among Internally Displaced Muslim Women in Puttalam, Sri Lanka. In Ahmed Ghosh, H. (ed.). *Walking the Tight Rope: Gender and Islam in Asia*. Albany: State University of New York Press. pp. 61–82.

Jeganathan, P. (2002) Walking Through Violence: Everyday life and Anthropology. In Mines, D. and Lamb, S. (eds.). *Everyday Life in South Asia*. Bloomington: Indiana University Press. pp. 357–365.

Lutz, C. (2002) The Wars Less Known. *The South Atlantic Quarterly*. 101 (2). pp. 285–296.

Staudt, K. and Mendez, Z. (2015) *Courage, Resistance and Women in Ciudad Juarez: Challenges to Militarization*. Austin: The University of Texas Press.

Strategic Foresight Group. (2006) *Cost of Conflict in Sri Lanka*. Mumbai: Strategic Foresight Group.

Tambiah, Y. (2004) Sexuality and Women's Rights in Armed Conflict in Sri Lanka. *Reproductive Health Matters*. 12 (23). pp. 78–87.

Tambiah, Y. (2005) Turncoat Bodies: Sexuality and Sex Work Under Militarization in Sri Lanka. *Gender and Society*. 19 (2). pp. 243–261.

Thiranagama, S. (2013) *In My Mother's House: Civil War in Sri Lanka*. Philadelphia: University of Pennsylvania Press.

Utas, M. (2005) Victimcy, Girlfriending, Soldiering: Tactic Agency in a Young Woman's Social Navigation of the Liberian War Zone. *Anthropological Quarterly* 78 (2). pp. 403–430.

Vigil, A. (2014) *War Echoes: Gender and Militarization in U.S. Latina/o Cultural Production*. New Jersey: Rutgers University Press.

Wijayatilake, K. (2004) *Study on Sexual and Gender Based Violence in Selected Locations in Sri Lanka*. Colombo: CENWOR.

Winslow, D. and Woost, M. (2004) Introduction. In Winslow, D. and Woost, M. (eds.). *Economy, Culture and Civil War in Sri Lanka*. Bloomington: Indiana University Press. pp. 1–31.

6 Guardians of girls

Policing and saving global workers in crises of love and sex

I was having an informal discussion with the Officer in Charge (OIC) of the Katunayake police station in 2008 when I received a call from Nita asking me to bring
Ms. Gamage, the female police sergeant in charge of the women's section, to the
NGO office where Nita worked. Apparently, Ms. Gamage was running late to a
workshop she was due to address at the NGO office. The OIC pointed toward the
back garden and said Ms. Gamage was bound to be in the smaller building across
the yard. When I was half way across the yard, the NGO driver blocked me and
asked that I go no further. For Ms. Gamage was giving two men accused of theft
a good beating. The mournful sounds emanating from the building did not make
me want to go any further in any case, and I returned to the NGO alone with a
rather amused driver.

Ms. Gamage did come to the NGO office about 20 minutes later and delivered her talk to a packed house of about 40 FTZ workers. It consisted solely of
advice to young women about how to comport themselves and behave with good
manners. She reiterated three times that they should never forget the good manners they internalized as village women. Her favorite words were *game hadiyawa*
(rural upbringing) and *gamikama* (ruralness). She condemned women for wearing makeup and blindly following fashions that invited bad men to make passes
at them, a comment that made me recall the time she looked at a handheld mirror
and applied powder on her face before posing for a photo with me.

"Many men tell us about the way garment girls come on to them. When bad
things happen to girls, and when it becomes clear that the girl provoked it, even
we face a dilemma about how to proceed," Ms. Gamage continued. Surprisingly,
the FTZ workers seemed to agree with her, and their questions after the talk were
not critical at all. At least two provided examples of other workers who, they
believed, behaved in too forward or brash a manner and provoked men to commit
violence: in one case, painfully pulling her hair and threatening to cut it and, in
the other, resorting to aggressive group fondling. These two responses, however,
prompted Ms. Gamage to blame the men and finally state that whatever women
do, men have no right to threaten and touch them violently. She asked the audience to report such incidents, whether they happened to them or anyone else, and
said that the police would see to it that the men would never ever think about
repeating such activities. Having overheard her punishing the two men accused of

theft, I did not doubt that she meant every word. What I doubted was the possibility that the workers would take their grievances to the police.

In accompanying factory workers to the Katunayake police station, I often witnessed the low regard the officers accorded them. Many workers complained that they were treated as whores when they visited the police station on routine matters and when out and about the FTZ area. This chapter examines the complex social class, gender, and nationalist implications associated with policing female garment workers by officers at the Katunayake and Seeduwa police stations. It also looks at the informal gaze and surveillance Air Force and Army contingents stationed around the FTZ, NGOs, and the neighbors direct at FTZ workers. The chapter argues that the tensions that occur when policing and disciplining get mired in nationalistic moral expectations complicate workers' already precarious lives. It further argues that police and other agents of surveillance are a significant part of the social class and gendered struggles that global workers daily engage in – spaces within which social identities and hierarchies are challenged and defended on spatial, appearance, and moral grounds. In short, these policing agents are partly responsible for the unutterability of premarital sexual desire and their ambivalent expressions and performances.

As noted throughout the book, women's migration has aroused deep anxieties over female morality and conduct. And moving from village to city for work allows women to jettison internalized sexual discipline and to articulate and negotiate new desires and pleasures. This empowerment exacerbates anxieties about female conduct, and many institutions and agents participate in an elaborate informal surveillance network focused on workers' lives. Elites, NGOs, and middle-class people simultaneously castigate the workers for their undisciplined behavior and desires; use them as a foil against which to assert their own moral and disciplined desires; and attempt to reform or "save" these women. For the workers themselves, it is precisely by pursuing these seemingly "undisciplined" desires that they enact and experience new forms of pleasure, empowerment, and selves. Women who faced violence within their relationships usually used local support systems – such as factory managers, the boarding house sisterhood, landladies, and ritual healers – before taking their problems to NGO support services and the police, who usually responded based on their understanding of ideal female behavior and social class practices.

Police officers, both male and female, are themselves poised between the working and middle classes and relish the opportunity to render their services in "saving wayward daughters." For example, in several cases, women who were victims of sexual assault, date rape, or statutory rape were disciplined for "moral transgressions" or "inappropriate behavior in public." This chapter thus also briefly focuses on the creative ways workers responded to these efforts to "save"' them while managing both their transgressions and reputations. The chapter, thus, extends the overall argument that nationalist concerns continue to reign when it comes to evaluating women's behavior and that attempts to both express and constrain different forms of desire are linked to the broader processes of global capitalism, nation-making, militarization, and constructions of the self.

Protectors of identities and hierarchies

> There is a conducive environment prevailing in Aweriwatte for a female to live with-
> out getting harmed, provided that she does not transgress the boundaries of decent
> behavior.

This is a quote from an abstract of a Master's thesis completed in 2004 by the then commander of the Katunayake Air force camp, Group Captain NHV Gunaratne. His thesis, while containing interesting statistics, reiterated the theme of female conduct by maintaining that if women workers avoid engaging in certain activities, such as going to musical shows or trips with males, they are bound to be personally secure. While some of the narratives in the thesis contradict this claim, the author concludes that "In view of the above findings, the hypothesis that the '(problems of) personal security of female factory workers are caused by their behavioral patterns' can be proved" (187). During my interviews with him he reiterated this and brought his subordinates who had dealt with workers to corroborate the claim that women themselves are responsible for provoking males to behave inappropriately or aggressively toward them. At the end of my field work that summer he presented me with a CD containing photos and audio recordings of his interviews as further evidence. Although the police officers did not have written statements, their actions, utterances, and ideas expressed in interviews made clear that they too considered women who had overstepped the boundaries of normative female conduct were responsible for the crimes committed against them.

Writing about a female semi-carceral correctional facility in Sri Lanka, Jody Miller and Carbone-Lopez show how the state controls women's perceived moral and sexual transgressions. They argue that the police operate under a highly unfair moral standard in that they consider it fine for them, as men, to seek the services of sex workers but strongly disapprove of women who transgress certain moral boundaries lest they become sex workers (2013). Tambiah (2004) explored an interesting fundamental rights court case filed by a male client who was arrested together with sex workers when the police raided the place. Although all the female sex workers were arrested, the reason for the raid, according to the police, was that they were looking for suspected LTTE cadres. Such gendered criminalization of moral transgressions is not a phenomenon peculiar to Sri Lanka. As shown earlier, varied officials in varied parts of the world sought to connect crimes committed against women to women's own transgressions of social and behavioral norms (Odem 1995). Many law enforcement officers and welfare personnel, especially at the turn of the last century, felt that moral transgressors deserved what befell them and some also felt that they should be punished further by being shamed and lectured on moral conduct (Alexander 1998; Enstad 1999). Writing about the significant role played by women officers of the London Metropolitan police in family and child welfare, Louise Jackson writes that they saw welfare and punishment as mutually reinforcing rather than conflicting concepts (2003).

Dray-Novey's work on the Beijing police during the Qing period concludes that their practices maintained the principles of social identity in pre-industrial urban China (1993). Most Western societies also record discriminatory treatment by police against poor, immigrant, marginalized, and racial minorities (Websdale and Johnson 2010; Fassin 2013). Similarly, this chapter shows that the so-called guardians of girls are in fact more concerned with maintaining a certain visual social order by keeping different groups of people in their place. Already marginalized as rural, poor, and female migrants, FTZ workers are placed at the bottom rung of society and were kept in that position through a series of linguistic, gestural, and interactional tools. Police and military are, in fact, major enforcers of this social order. Most officers' routine conflation of laws with rules of conduct, and their concerns with ideal female behavior, help maintain the existing social order by further stigmatizing and criminalizing migrant global factory workers.

Transgress once and we punish twice

During my long term association with FTZ women workers I have had many occasions to observe interactions between workers and police. Lower ranked constables made fun and tried to attract workers' attention on the street, but when at the police station they treated workers mostly with disrespect borne out of class, gender, and FTZ work-related prejudices. Their treatment of female workers varied according to the complaint, and many complaints were prejudged using popular media accounts of FTZ workers as village women who get into trouble due to their own weak-heartedness and stupidity.

For instance, in 2000 I accompanied two workers, one of whom wished to make an entry about losing her national identity card, to the police station. The first thing the desk clerk, a male cop, said was "Ah, so the lover boy stole your purse with the ID card?" Sunethra, who had come to the FTZ about two months before and did not have a boyfriend, burst into tears on our way back to the boarding house. Her purse with some hard-earned cash, ID card, and her late mother's photo had been stolen in a crowded bus, and now she rightly felt doubly injured. She again burst into tears at the boarding house, and the workers present shared their own experiences of being verbally abused for moral wrong-doings police and others generally associated with FTZ workers. They grumbled about how police personnel made assumptions whenever they went to the station: if they complained about losing something, it was because their boyfriends (whom they were not supposed to have) stole the items; if they complained about boarding mistress throwing them out, it was because they ran around town with men and did not go back at reasonable times; if they complained about men who cheated them out of money, it was because they jumped into bed with them like common whores. Although they laughed when acting out these scenarios, it was obvious that they were pained by such treatment and wished it would not occur. Some of them even pleaded with me to intercede on their behalf.

On separate occasions, workers recounted incidents where women who had been victims of sexual assault, date rape, or statutory rape were disciplined for "moral transgressions" or "inappropriate behavior in public." In a case I was involved in an advisory capacity, a 14-year-old worker "eloped" with her older boyfriend. After the parents complained, the couple was found and brought to the police station. The woman officer in charge, Ms. Gamage, started the interrogation by beating the young girl for behaving badly. Although the issue should have been treated as a statutory abduction and rape case, given that the age of consent in Sri Lanka is 16, the officer put the blame on the girl, claiming her bad behavior in pursuing a boyfriend at such a young age was the main cause for this outcome.

Even when police verbal and physical abuse were not so conspicuous, officers' behavior made clear that they nonchalantly conflated penal and moral codes. On two occasions, I accompanied several workers when they went to visit a military deserter who had been a resident at Saman's boarding house for a few months before being arrested and placed in remand custody at the police station. Nihal had been living with a 17-year-old worker, and a week before the arrest dumped her to start a relationship with another young worker. The whole week he slept with her and when her enraged parents came to forcibly take the young woman home, they reported him as a military deserter.

Although his conduct at the boarding house was highly criticized, many women residents visited him in his cell and shed tears. On both occasions several police officers disparagingly mocked the young women for their stupidity, vulgarity, and sluttiness. They claimed that about 15 women had come and cried, saying Nihal was their boyfriend. The second time I was there, an officer judged that I was not a factory worker (probably by my clothes and the way I stayed back, somewhat bemused at the emotional display) and gave an impassioned speech about misbehaving factory workers. According to him, officers preferred not to be stationed in Katunayake because, in addition to engaging in standard police activities, they felt burdened by having to protect weak and wrongheaded women workers from getting into all sorts of scrapes. "We need more women police officers who can advise these girls on how to behave in Colombo. They have lived like prisoners with their parents, and here they are running amok. They do not understand how their actions affect their futures as well as our Sinhala Buddhist culture," he complained. "Now this man is married and has a wife and two kids in his village. He came here after getting six months' salary because he knew he could befriend girls easily. He had girlfriends in many boarding houses in the area. Do you think that all he did with them was walk on the railroad tracks hand-in-hand eating ice cream cones? No, he came here because his wife is now fat and ugly with children hanging onto her, and he needed a new taste," the elderly policeman continued.

Meanwhile, the other policemen used such words as *thamusela, oyi,* and *isela* (disrespectful address forms) to disperse the women while commenting on their immorality. One young cop yelled, "*Yanawala oyi gewal walata. Meka malageyak newei, Thamusela magule gihilla badawal handagaththata policiya pali nehe* (Go home, women. This is not a funeral home. If you had sex and now have pregnant bellies, what can the police do?). None of the women present were pregnant or claimed that Nihal seduced them. They lived in other rooms of the same boarding house as Nihal and thought it was their duty to visit him. Although many were shedding tears, the policeman had no reason to so hastily connect their visiting and tears with unwanted pregnancies. The police, at least the ones involved in these cases, seemed to think that these women had already "transgressed" by migrating to cities or finding boyfriends, and it was therefore alright for them to be humiliated verbally and/or physically.

Two stories of lost gold bangles

Two stories pertaining to lost bangles underline how important the image that a worker cultivates at the FTZ can be when dealing with varied agents of control. A good image that has been validated through interconnected institutions (i.e., factory and boarding house) that suggests a FTZ worker is hardworking, obedient, and docile plays to her advantage even among police personnel. Vasanthi was one such worker who had earned a "good girl certificate" both at the factory and the boarding house. She was boarded at her brother-in law's parents' house in Katunayake together with her then best friend. One day the latter borrowed four gold bangles from Vasanthi saying she had to go to a wedding. Thereafter she moved to another boarding house and refused to return the bangles.

Vasanthi, a diligent worker whose good looks had led to her being picked as the factory beauty queen the year before, told her personnel manager what had taken place while explaining why she had been absent from work. Realizing that they were losing the full attention of a good worker due to the theft, the manager wrote a letter to the OIC and sent Vasanthi and her aunt-in-law in the factory van to the police station. The personnel manager's letter, factory van, and the elderly female relative all caused Vasanthi to have a very different experience at the police station from what I usually witnessed. They were seated, listened to, and promised a speedy resolution. Three days later she was asked to come to the police station via a phone call to the personnel office, which dispatched her to the police station in the factory van. The ex-roommate was already there with two of Vasanthi's bangles and had written a letter promising to pay her for the other two bangles within two months. The woman was crying when Vasanthi reached the police station, because police officers took turns berating her. The verbal abuse continued even after Vasanthi got to the station. The berating was less for the theft and more for learning from all her secret lovers (*hora minissungen*) how to steal hardworking women's jewelry. The words used to berate her were too obscene for Vasanthi to repeat, and she was shocked. Vasanthi and her friends agreed that the woman was wrong to steal, but they also felt it was unnecessary to accuse her of secret lovers given that it was most probably a family emergency that may have caused the women to do what she did.

Devika also lost two bangles, but what ensued following this theft was much different from Vasanthi's experience. When Devika was a resident at Saman's boarding house they were supposedly in a relationship involving sexual intercourse. During this time Saman borrowed two of her bangles, which he then pawned. A few months later Saman found another girlfriend and forced Devika out. He kept promising to settle the loan associated with the bangles for about two years, even as he assured Devika he was going to get rid of the other girl, thus giving her hopes of reconciliation. One day financial and emotional pressures came to a head and Devika started shouting in front of Saman's house threatening to commit suicide if he did not return her bangles. She also kept looking toward the main road and, when Saman threatened physical violence, screamed that she had telephoned the police station and the cops were going to be coming soon. She thereafter showed him a bottle of pesticide and said, "As the police jeep arrives I am going to drink poison in front of Mr. Inspector and then you (Saman) will get a different kind of bangles (handcuffs)." At this Saman jumped out of the house and started hitting Devika, who fell to the ground wailing. No police jeep came by and Devika was led away by other workers.

I am not sure if Devika actually telephoned the police or believed someone was bound to call the authorities if she made sufficient noise. According to workers with whom I witnessed her breakdown, it was unlikely that Devika would have lodged a complaint because that would have revealed she had engaged in sexual relations with Saman. They also agreed that even if she had complained, the police would not have taken any action because there was no proof such as a signed letter/receipt and because they would have considered it her fault for acting promiscuously and parting with her bangles without proof because of love/lust.

Vasanthi too lacked any signed document but her "good girl" character led to justice being implemented. Loaning the bangles to a female friend and being certified as a "good girl" by the factory personnel manager and an elderly relative made the difference in the two cases. When I recounted the two incidents to a new OIC at the police station, he acknowledged that he too would have considered a letter from a factory official and an accompanying relative positively. He also said that if Devika had gone to the police station in time and had provided witnesses, she too would have received speedy attention. He further agreed that if he had to make a choice between the two cases due to lack of personnel or vehicles, which he claimed was always the case, he would have been more inclined to take up Vasanthi's case.

I will discuss later how the women workers themselves negotiated the good girl/bad girl images. At this point it is important to note the social class struggles that color these interactions, choices, and responses. While both constables and officers generally held similar ideas about social norms, transgressions, discipline, and punishment, there were some notable differences in the way the two groups negotiated power, duty, and obligations. The following section briefly discusses the complex class negotiations enacted through creating and protecting boundaries and identities.

Class boundary struggles

Workers understood that the officers belonged to upper class families (*loku pawul-wala*), and they usually uncritically accepted the latter's superior comportment. But they had a hard time reconciling the put downs of constables. Indeed, workers told me they were most hurt when constables insulted and abused them because such individuals often came from villages like their own and they felt they ought to try and appreciate their plight/challenges. "They must have sisters like us. They treat us nicely, tease and joke with us on foot patrol, but put on airs when we see them at the station. It is like the station assigns them more power when they are inside," Malika once lamented. Workers haven't quite figured the reasons for this disparity, but their experiences suggested that constables were trying to impress their superiors and also prove allegiance to middle class moral codes. It was only after I got to know more about recruitment and promotion patterns that I realized why class mobility and protecting certain moral norms were important for both constables and officers.

While constables are recruited mostly from among the urban and rural poor and under educated youth who often have only passed the GCE O/L exam, officers come from more middle class homes, often have university degrees, or have excelled in sports while at high school. While some do come from the lower middle class, some are from upper middle class homes. The internal promotional structure, however, allows constables to be promoted to sergeant, sub-inspector, and even inspector, although most achieve the latter two promotions when they are close to retirement. Levels of education, English-speaking ability, and appearance generally differed between those who had been recruited directly as officers and those who attained the position through promotions. At the Katunayake police station, just as in other stations, constables' desire to get promoted in no small measure contributed to their aping officers' proclivities when dealing with those from working classes, and this was mainly why constables were cruder when dealing with women workers within the police station premises.

I formally interviewed three OICs and also conducted a few informal discussions with them and two other officers attached to the Katunayake and Seeduwa police stations. In 2000 the OIC of Katunayake was one Mr. Jayasiri, who hailed from Kandy and was in his mid-fifties. He was recruited as a constable but had risen through the ranks to reach the post of sub-inspector. He was tall, skinny, and balding and had a tendency to walk around the station without shoes. He definitely considered protecting women part of his duty and tantamount to protecting the Sinhala culture. His everyday conversations were peppered with concerns about the nation and how important it was for women to safeguard the nation's good name. His biggest concern pertained to a group of women who lived as couples in a boarding house. These women workers apparently shared a public well with other area residents who were upset by their unbecoming behavior and complained to the police. "These girls bathe around 11:00 p.m. and midnight wearing just panties and all the airport vans park around the well to see this spectacle," Mr. Jayasiri complained. Without ever using the Sinhala word for homosexuality, he alluded to lesbian activities and used his eyes and hands to convey his feelings of shock and revulsion. Perhaps suspecting that I might not be able to read his facial and hand gestures, he went on to say that he and a group of cops twice raided the house and were shocked to find some women wearing sarongs and sleeping together within the same sarong. This was again done while making exasperated facial expressions. Although I realized that he was referring to lesbianism as a crime, I asked if such behavior was illegal in any way. This caused him to look confused. Thankfully, Nita, who accompanied me to the station that day, strategically changed the conversation by bringing up his raids on illegal abortion clinics in Seeduwa and Ja-Ela, both nearby towns. He once more went on about how these clinics were destroying young migrant women workers and that he would not rest until he had gotten rid of all abortion clinics in the area. When I asked what women should do if they find themselves with an unwanted pregnancy, Mr. Herat replied, "They should think about that before going down the wrong path. If they did wrong things, they have to suffer the consequences."

By 2006, Sub-inspector Jayasiri had been transferred to Kandy, and Inspector De Pinto had taken over as the OIC. He was tall, well-built, in his forties, and insisted on speaking to me in English. He clearly enjoyed speaking in a very official way and seemed to be well-versed in the country's laws. His main goal, he said, was to eliminate the "sexual harassment virus" pervading the FTZ. He personally went after men who catcalled and whistled at women or followed them in groups. He and Nita both talked with glee about the time he heard a three-wheeler driver cat-calling at a group of women. Nita was in the jeep with him, traveling to an official NGO meeting, and said that Mr. De Pinto stopped the three-wheeler, pulled the driver out by his shirt collar, slapped him twice, and shoved him into the back of the jeep. Although Nita sounded awe-struck by this display of authority, she also said later that the FTZ workers the three-wheeler driver had directed his comments to did not seem to appreciate the harsh treatment meted out to someone who, according to them, was having innocent fun. As noted earlier, women workers do not begrudge such men who engage in catcalling and often took pleasure in being singled out.

When I asked Mr. De Pinto about sexual harassment sentencing he said there was no need to try these men as all they needed to know was that the police were keeping an eye on them and will not tolerate such boorish behavior. At this point I told him that my research was showing that workers were not wholly opposed to catcalls as this allowed men to express an interest in them. Inspector De Pinto started speaking in Sinhalese and asked me to think of all the unwanted pregnancies, abortions, and suicides around the area and the image this created among foreigners about Sri Lankan culture. "Do you think a good man would catcall a woman and follow them in groups? Would you like to marry such a man? When I wanted to befriend my wife I asked her at the church, and then she invited me to come to her house and talk to her parents. That's the proper path. Rapes and abortions won't happen if the beginning is good," he said. When I pointed out that workers reported that many men who catcalled and whistled were police and military men stationed around the FTZ and the airport, he replied that his boys had reported that workers typically provoked them into saying something. He, however, asked me to note down the badge number of such cops and report to him if I witnessed such incidents and he promised to punish them severely.

Unlike Mr. Jayasiri, Mr. De Pinto had been recruited as an officer after he had passed his GCE (A/L) exams. He was also quite successful in several sports at a well-known Catholic school. Both men took kindly to FTZ workers, albeit in a chauvinistic manner. They were concerned about women's welfare and were ready to punish both the women workers and men who harass them to save other innocent workers. Mr. Jayasiri deliberately projected an image of an elderly father figure who was concerned about naïve girls. Mr. De Pinto seemed more thoroughly absorbed in classed notions that suggested "these women had to be controlled because it is in their nature to be raunchy and unruly." While they both maintained the class boundaries through their language and actions, they did not have to go out of their way to create boundaries as their very position created the boundary at several levels.

This was even more pronounced in the case of Mr. Wijesinghe, who became the OIC in 2008. He was a tall, fair man in his early thirties, with a university degree. He joined the police force directly as a sub-inspector and was promoted to full rank within two years. He was uncomfortable with all the additional responsibilities associated with Katunayake's heavy female migrant population, and when Ms. Gamage was transferred from Gampaha to Katunayake, in mid-2008 to head the women's section, he gladly allowed her to oversee all women-related matters. Nita especially found it interesting that the OIC of the Katunayake police station tried to stay away from matters relating to the female workforce. I hung out at the police station frequently during 2009 as Mr. Wijesinghe proved much more supportive of my research endeavors than his two predecessors. He and the other policemen liked to talk to me about the U.S. and my work, and this gave me ample opportunity to also observe the interactions between FTZ workers and the police. All crimes and complaints were reported to the OIC but many worker complaints were sent directly to Ms. Gamage for further action. Once in a while he murmured his frustration over the sorts of complaints workers lodged, which typically dealt with men and other women who had cheated them. He once said his biggest pet peeve was the way women started to weep and wail without coherently stating the problem. "I am embarrassed by such behavior. I feel very lucky that Ms. Gamage is here to take care of these women. You have seen her, right? She knows how to control these women."

I especially appreciated him sending me to Ms. Gamage's office and, on a few occasions, letting me sit in his office when he felt the issue at hand was bound to interest me. One day in summer 2009, Mr. Wijesinghe called in a young woman who had been picked up the night before. Assuming that I might be in the office to help her, the woman started to tell me what happened. But the OIC stopped her in an uncharacteristically rough manner and said she was brought there for me to observe her and not for her to ramble on. He then told me that she was sleeping with seven men in a rooming house and that all eight had been arrested. The young woman interrupted again to say that she had gone to a musical show with a male friend and since it ended late she agreed to stay at his boarding house, which he shared with six other men. "They were in their rooms. We did not do anything wrong," she pleaded. Annoyed at her interruption, the OIC asked a cop to take her to Ms. Gamage for a lesson. When I asked why she was arrested, he looked at me and reiterated the above story, attempting one or two sentences in English, supposedly to make it easy for me to understand.

This incident showed me that he too had internalized the dominant cultural notions of what constituted respectable womanly behavior and applied it while carrying out his duties. It is possible that his well-known dislike of dealing with emotional women workers and aversion to physical punishment were unconscious means that created a class boundary at a separate level: the benign gentleman who abhorred any excess. And yet it was excess – specifically related to police brutality – that caused Mr. Wijesinghe's exit from Katunayake in 2011. He, Ms. Gamage, and nearly all personnel in the station were transferred after police fired on an anti-government protest by FTZ workers, killing one and injuring many others.

It is my duty as a woman to direct them along the correct path

Cecilia MacDowell Santos's 2005 book, titled *Female Only Police Stations in Brazil*, examines police stations run exclusively by women officers authorized to investigate crimes against women, such as domestic violence, assault, and rape. She investigates the political implications of these stations even while exploring gendered citizenship. While this is a positive new development, in many ways the book is focused on the relationship between women police and the state and does not pay attention to interactions at the ground level and class complications.

This is important to explore as many in the police force seem to think that as long as there is a women's section with some female officers, women's problems are well taken care of. As indicated above with Mr. Wijesinghe and his reliance on Ms. Gamage for all things woman-related, such situations can have negative consequences depending on the female officers' ambitions and particular ideological and class positioning.

Ms. Gamage, by all accounts, is a very capable, efficient, and fearless female officer. She is of formidable appearance, so much so that Nita told me that she too feels like crying when she sees her. The first time Nita took me to see Ms. Gamage, she insisted on my buying a particularly expensive box of biscuits as a gift. It turned out to be a prudent choice as Ms. Gamage softened considerably after we presented the gift. However, at first, she did not seem to approve of my looks and the bumbling way in which I explained why I had visited the police station. She was in her early forties, heavy set, tall, with an intimidating stance, and lived about 12 miles from Katunayake with her family. When dealing with working class people, both men and women, she was heavy handed and foul mouthed. As the OIC was uncomfortable with any physical punishment, he left her in charge of beating all suspected wrong-doers, both men and women. She relished this power and, according to many reports, was quite adept at administering brutal physical assaults. Both Nita and I felt that even the young OIC was somewhat intimidated by her.

The vignette with which I started this chapter amply evidenced Gamage's take on women workers and their troubles. Although she herself did not act according to the norms of a respectable Sinhala Buddhist woman, she vigorously drew from discourses surrounding good womanly behavior when dealing with young

FTZ workers. A conversation I had with Gamage about the 14-year-old worker who eloped showed that she believed workers who broke social norms deserved no sympathy. When I was visiting another former worker in Dutuwawa, a town about 20 miles from the city of Anuradhapura, this young woman and her mother, having travelled quite a distance, came to visit me. The mother was outraged by the way Ms. Gamage had beaten her teenage daughter saying the young woman was so humiliated for being accused of something she did not do, she left her job at the FTZ. Thereafter she ate little and lost interest in everything around her. The mother wanted to know whether I could do something about the unfair treatment meted out to her child, who she claimed had been taken away against her will.

When I later met with Ms. Gamage I inquired about this underaged girl being beaten. She reacted angrily and complained that NGO people and activists like me only knew how to criticize police practices, without appreciating the trying conditions under which they worked. She said that after the complaint was made she and her colleagues had to drop everything they were doing and go from house to house looking for this girl who developed the poison of desire (*magul vise*) before even coming out of the seed pod (before even blossoming into woman-hood). It was imperative that the young girl was taught a lesson so she would never do this sort of thing again, and Mrs. Gamage said she also wanted to use the woman to deter others like her. She emphasized that it was her duty as a woman and mother to show these young women the correct path. Her outburst scared me enough to question her no further. Noticing how perturbed I was by her outburst, she explained, in a more conciliatory tone, why keeping young women's behavior in check, preventing premarital sex, and punishing wrong-doers were important. "We have a responsibility toward these girls' parents. The future of the country and the culture are in these girls' hands, and if they go the wrong way, the whole country is done for."

I often wondered why it was so important for a woman who, by her demeanor and physical actions, did not adhere to norms of ideal womanly comportment demanded such conformity in FTZ workers. Although her demeanor and police activities were not normative, she followed the normative path in some ways. She got into an arranged marriage, had three children, and traveled to work from her home. By 2008 she had been promoted to sergeant, but Ms. Gamage had been recruited as a constable due to her educational level. Her husband worked as a minor employee at a private company. She, therefore, was precari-ously positioned between the working and middle classes. It is easy to see how nationalist discourses pertaining to the nation's purity and protection during a time of war can influence the thinking and behavior of the likes of Ms. Gamage. Additionally, the emphasis on nation and female morality provided her ample opportunities to play up to middle class sensibilities and thereby delineate class boundaries. As she once told me, "however much we try, we cannot make these women like us. It is their way. They haven't had a good upbringing and they put black marks on their parents, us and the country." Generalizations about FTZ workers' transgressions provided Ms. Gamage with many tools to create differ-ence and otherness.

Not all women police officers were as unkind as Ms. Gamage when dealing with FTZ workers. While the few at the station yelled and generally looked down on workers, none of them beat workers and were shocked when they first encountered Ms. Gamage doing so. I met Ranjula, a female constable attached to *Diri Piyasa* (House of Courage), a community outreach center of the Ministry of Women's Affairs, in Katunayake in 2005. She had been in the service for three years and had spent close to a year at the center by then. I visited with her many times during 2005–2007 and conducted an in-depth interview in 2006.

Ranjula said she chose to become a police woman because of the social status the job accorded. She liked looking smart in the police uniform and the stable income. Ranjula was certain that her job automatically placed her in a higher social rank than the workers. However, she spoke kindly of them and said she understood the feelings of loneliness they experienced and why they may seek protection through boyfriends as she also was an unmarried young woman from a rural village who lived in a boarding house. "This job and this uniform give me a lot of courage and strength. Workers don't have that, and they foolishly think that having a boyfriend frees them of unwanted attention. That works if the boyfriend is an honest man. If not, there are problems related to unwanted pregnancies and abortions. You must have heard about the woman who threw her newborn baby out of the second floor window. I blame the parents. How come they didn't know the daughter was pregnant. Perhaps they did not visit her for nine months. When they let young, sheltered women loose like this, what can they expect? These are human beings. They fall for quick pleasures." This younger, migrant police woman's response was somewhat different from Ms. Gamage's and might stem from her being attached to a center instituted to help and care for workers in trouble.

According to Ranjula and two other female police women, their job was to make those who came to the center feel comfortable about going to the police, and they partly did so by trying to convince the women that there was no legal remedy to whatever their problems without a formal entry being made. The police women said many workers associate police stations with male cops and are therefore ashamed about lodging entries pertaining to sexual harassment, rape, or other gender-based violence. And so they go to NGOs hoping to talk to women. The center was created with the hope of trying to change this attitude. They said women workers came from surrounding areas to discuss sexual assault and conflicts involving family and finances and that they usually advised and encouraged them to make complaints at their area police station. The two other police women I talked to at this particular center spoke to the workers kindly and respectfully but did not show much interest in their plight and held them responsible, almost single handedly, for their problems. As one woman noted, "Ranjula and I are from remote villages too. Just like them we have migrated for work. Why cannot they manage their jobs, personal lives and finances like us? It is because of foolishness, lack of education and neglect by their parents." She also mentioned the obscene magazines they read and named several that I have never heard of, such as *Lick of Fire, Bambara, Susara, Senuri*, and *Sewwandi*. "You can look high and low, but someone like you will never find these bad magazines. Traders know their clientele and will only sell to garment workers," she continued.

Although they were respectful and did help workers to negotiate the law's intricacies, all three, to varied extents, seemed to hold workers as less-disciplined and, therefore, less respectable. Their different demeanor and behavior, compared to that of Ms. Gamage, was likely genuine, but it is unclear how they may have responded to women who visited the police station (as opposed to the center). After all, these are women who are using a government job to move up socially – and expressing and acting on nationalist and militaristic gendered duties and responsibilities are common tools of transcending class boundaries on the way up.

NGO female staff and the neighbors

Several NGOs assisted women through labor and personal problems. The interactions I witnessed made clear that NGO workers were respectful and kind when dealing with the workers and their problems. Most NGO staff members thrived on having individual cases to work on and took to some cases with passion and dedication. In the case of Sachini (described in Chapter 2), two NGO staff members helped her file a lawsuit against the father of the baby and accompanied her to the courts. The man first claimed that she slept with many people and the baby was not his. The NGO paid for the lawyers and the paternity test, which proved he was indeed the father. Then he petitioned the courts for full custody of the baby claiming she was not fit to be a mother and that he feared she would spend the child support on her own pleasures. Outraged female staff, with the help of a well-known human rights lawyer, challenged his claim in the courts. This last triumph occurred after I had left to return to the United States and the staff crowed about it for months via email.

However, things changed by the following summer. The staff found definitive proof that the man was correct about the woman's promiscuous behavior. They were appalled that they helped such an immoral woman who was running around with men, without focusing adequately on her baby, and at least one staff member wanted to help the father get full custody. However, the ruckus they made the previous year about Sachini being a young woman pressured for sex by a man made the NGO helpless. Group discussions within the NGO evidenced deep belief in normative good behavior for women and the forgivable mistakes of not so educated women. All three female and two male staff members present at this discussion held that the baby should be taken from Sachini as she hardly was an innocent girl who had fallen for the lies of an opportunistic man, but someone who went looking for trouble and continued to act irresponsibly.

The fact that I did not meet NGO members who did not hold deeply held notions about female conduct does not mean that such individuals do not exist. Most NGO workers are kind, well-meaning people who have not thought through their own entrapment within normative structures of behavior. The workers I met at this same NGO were shocked to hear of Sachini's behavior and thought such women put a black mark on everyone working in the FTZ. Writing about the paradoxical roles that the Dagongmei's Home, a Beijing women's organization that promotes the rights and interests of female migrants, plays in producing identities for its members and in channeling their voices into the public arena, Fu (2009) notes that the organization is both a site of articulation and a cage that constrains the voices of migrant women. According to Fu (2009), since the migrant women only can speak as members of the NGO, they end up reproducing the government discourses on development and modernization. Similarly, although most FTZ NGOs allow workers space to voice their grievances against factories and labor and living conditions, they can only speak within the ideological universes of the NGOs shaping their voices. This situation lead to women's deeply held beliefs about normative and transgressive behaviors being reinforced, or their staying away from NGOs altogether.

Neighbors

Neighbors, especially the boarding aunties, were vigilant when it came to the behavior of their own boarders and workers who frequented their neighborhoods. Many had unwritten rules and preferences about who they wanted as renters. It was common for them to not want to rent rooms to couples and to women who came looking for rooms without family. Some did not want women who came home after dark (usually 6:00 p.m.), while one boarding house owner said she did not rent to women who came with grandmothers. When I asked this particular landlady why she did not like girls brought up by grandmothers she said, "There has to be a reason why the mother left the child with her mother. Unwanted pregnancy, elopement, divorce . . . whatever it is, she could not be a good woman. And the reason she was like that was because her own mother did not bring her up well. So how can this grandmother bring the granddaughter up well? Fruits of a tree do not fall far from the tree, you know. I don't want such girls to corrupt these other good girls."

While many boarding house owners claim to care about women's good behavior and say they are committed to protecting the culture and nation by policing women workers, they are not averse to compromising these positions for financial gain. By 2015, six years after the end of the war, the FTZ had attracted a significant number of Tamil workers from North and East Provinces and tea estates in Central Province. Unlike Sinhala young men, male estate Tamils have found FTZ employment to be much more attractive than opportunities available on tea estates. They have therefore accompanied girlfriends, sisters, and wives to the area. The few boarding houses that accommodate these workers have consequently initiated new rules, such as checking marriage certificates and keeping brothers and sisters in separate rooms. These individuals cook and eat together, but their sex dictates where they sleep. Their boarding owners claimed that they did not let unmarried couples share rooms, while one owner said she did not even let them stay in the same complex. The government-run model female hostel, which housed a number of Tamil workers, did not accept married couples and the two matrons even prohibited men from visiting the women on the premises.

More often than not, the long-time residents who built houses and acquired middle-class accoutrements by engaging in informal economic activities related to the FTZ assert their supposed good morals and discipline by attempts to reform or "save" these women. They complain to the police about women workers' "immoral" activities, and thereby claim to be "good citizens" who protect culture by controlling women workers' misguided behavior. Some older boarding aunties told me that they frequently called the police when they saw couples glued together in back alleys and dark places. During the civil war, police sometimes used emergency laws (and thin canes) to disperse lovers talking at street corners. In 2013 one landlady said she was planning to get people to sign a petition so that the thin canes could be brought back. According to her, being caned caused no physical pain but shamed those misbehaving. "That's what they need for these shameless activities – a good lesson to never do it again." Her intention here, she said, was to save the uncorrupted, obedient girls and stop them from emulating the shameless, corrupted ones.

It is of interest that while mainstream Buddhist religious rituals play a big role in the lives of global factory workers, no woman I talked to felt that male monks in nearby temples treated them differently because they were FTZ workers. No one said that they were being used negatively by monks to encourage others toward a more moral lifestyle. When it came to temple sermons the women generally felt that they differed little from what they heard in their villages. And while they found older monks to be kind but somewhat aloof, they felt the younger monks were at times a bit too friendly. This is not surprising, given that some young monks at nearby temples have been known to disrobe thanks to romances with FTZ workers.

While Buddhist monks, unlike police personnel, boarding house owners, factory managers, and some NGO officials did not make workers feel ashamed or devalued, workers did not seek the help of clergy when dealing with angst stemming from losing one's virginity, pregnancy, and abortions. They instead went to ritual specialists and thereby created a somewhat symbiotic relationship with those who engaged in folk supernaturalism. It appears that women felt they could not count on mainstream institutional or religious support during such periods of crisis and that they felt more comfortable among a marginalized religious outlet.

This led ritual specialists and shrines to proliferate as part of another FTZ commercial enterprise. What was striking was that some of these practitioners seemed genuinely concerned and protective of their young female clientele. Several ritual specialists kept case books, but no one allowed me to read any entries even after I assured them I would not use people's real names. This suggested they cared for these workers and had a locally shaped understanding of safe-guarding their clients' reputations. As one ritual specialist noted, "When I hear of a suicide attempt I check my book and see whether it is one of my girls."

None of the ritual specialists I talked to said anything about women inviting trouble on themselves by transgressing gender and sexual norms. On the one hand, these women's troubles were the source of their income. On the other hand, they, as ritual specialists, had seen people from all social strata facing similar troubles and secretively seeking supernatural help while publicly denigrating such practices. When I told one healer how a police officer I talked to said that the state institutions are not responsible for providing services when women misbehave and get into trouble, he somewhat angrily said, "It is easy for him to say those things but if his daughter gets into trouble then it is to us he would have to come too." At a focus group discussion, Nimali, a FTZ worker, said that one reason women run to these shrines and ritual specialists is because their services are cheap and easily available. "Women don't like to go to NGOs with their troubles because they (staff) start preaching and behaving like they are born of flowers (very pure/better than us)," Shirani explained. "These ritual specialists are poor people as we are. They make a living by us and do not look down on us or laugh at us," Nimali further added (Hewamanne 2010). Although the discussion showed that ritual healers are bright spots in crises situations, it also shows how government and non-government institutions neatly stay uninvolved in catering to the legal, emotional and physical needs of the FTZ worker population, if such needs arise from what they considered moral transgressions. Although these institutions are legally, or as stated in their mission statements, bound to help women in crises, the ongoing narrative of "good women would not have premarital sex" keeps women away from their premises and instead makes it necessary for them to go to ritual healers.

Workers' responses: "We are forced to lie and pretend"

Saman married Chuti just two years before he died (in 2012), although they had lived together for about 10 years prior to that. Three days after the funeral, Saman's mother threw Chuti out of the house saying that the marriage was a sham and the certificate bogus. Within two days Chuti realized that Saman had cheated her by taking her through a fake civil ceremony. I was not in Sri Lanka when this happened and, therefore, I called her in July 2013 to offer condolences and to encourage her to take legal action. She was under no illusions as to how the police or the courts would hear the case. "Miss, you know my history. Both my older sisters lived with him before me. At one time all three of us were his women. And then I lived with him for 10 more years without getting married. If I go to the police, his mother would divulge all this, and the police would call me a whore and kick me out of the police station. Not even a lawyer would take my case – they would think I don't deserve justice as I have shamed all good women in this country." However saddened, I had to respect her decision, knowing that she had only a very slim chance of winning a case against Saman's mother. In the eyes of police and society "good girls do not live with men," and even her being tricked into a fake marriage was bound to fall on deaf ears.

As I noted earlier in the chapter, women complained about the way police treated them and tried to stay away from the police if at all possible. They were not able to clearly articulate the connections of social class boundaries, class moralities, and dominant norms, yet they knew they were being unfairly treated and resented it. Perhaps it is this resentment that brought forth some creative ways of responding to the efforts at "saving" them. Acting like innocent victims who were deceived by opportunistic and evil men was the most effective and respectable option when attracting attention to their cases. Crying, weeping, and fainting also helped. Shamini once told me that she would not tell the police that she willingly had sex even if it is the case or that she gave her necklace to a man because she loved him. "I would say that I was raped or that he broke the chain right off of my neck. Who wants to hear their obscene words?" There were about ten workers present at the boarding room at this time and they admonished her to be careful with such statements. All of them agreed that it is wrong to lie to the police. But they also agreed that sometimes they just do not have any other options.

"It is like they want us, no expect us – in the name of our wonderful culture – to lie. To tell them that we are not 'bad' women, so they can treat us like foolish, yet good girls and help us." This comment from Hemamali led to a long discussion on society's hypocrisies, which led to us all pitching in with stories of lying to our parents, teachers and neighbors because doing so made everyone feel better.

One day in 2012 when Rangika was prepping a newer worker about how to visit the police station I heard her asking the latter to carry her documents inside a *Sandarajini* magazine instead of a plastic bag. When I later inquired about the reasons for this suggestion she said that when she once went to the police station with her ID card and money tucked within an old *Sandarajini* magazine two policemen commented that it was good to see FTZ girls reading this sort of magazine as opposed to obscene magazines (*Priyadari, Bambara* etc.). I could not help but connect this again with the class aspirations I discussed earlier. *Sandarajini* and *Bhavana*, while considered silly tabloid reads, in fact represent romances within normative structures. It also represents a reconciliation of the policemen's nationalist loyalties and class aspirations. In their eyes workers who read such material were good girls who are not too corrupt, but also not of the same class as good novel reading government servants such as them.

Women workers are savvy enough to know what makes them come across as good girls and so they play along. On the one hand, it is a tragedy that they have to play these classed and gendered games to get basic services that all citizens are entitled to. On the other hand, this play let them manage their transgressions by actively manipulating people's sentiments. This is similar to the way they manipulated the surveillance network around the FTZ to manage their reputations in the villages. For instance, workers tell those in their villages about police, NGOs and neighborhood surveillance mechanisms to indicate that they are just as protected in the city as in the village. They specifically utilize boarding house owners in this regard, claiming that their boarding aunties are stricter than their parents and that sometimes they feel more protected in the city than in the villages due to their vigilance. During my repeated visits to their native villages, I realized that their parents also used the police and neighborhood supervision to manage their daughters' reputations.

Political economy, nationalism, and surveillance

Since 2000, the Sri Lanka Police Department has worked closely with the Women's Affairs Ministry to conduct sensitivity training for police officers regarding sexual harassment and general comportment. According to some experienced NGO officers, they are seeing a difference in the way some police officers behave and speak. However, none of the incidents described in the early part of this chapter, except for illegal abortion clinics, violate the Sri Lanka penal code. As noted earlier, conflating official duties with policing and punishing garment workers' private behavior stem from a broader understanding about women's morality being deeply connected to the purity and honor of the nation and culture. While it is understandable for there to have been high surveillance in general during the civil war, the fact that this surveillance continues post-civil war proves that it had little to do with the ethnic conflict to begin with. FTZ workers were always monitored, but that was not because neighbors and the state worried about their being attacked by the LTTE; it was because they desired to control their activities, which they equated with national and cultural purity.

This monitoring and disciplining created differences between the workers and long-time residents and police, who themselves are somewhat precariously positioned between the working and middle classes. Two questions encompass the empirical data in this chapter. How do surveillance, punishing, and efforts to save women connect to the political economy of transnational production? Are there connections between what agents of surveillance do and the basic structural needs of transnational production? While one may not be able to explicitly point to such connections, I contend that the particular configuration of surveillance and punishment has been influenced by specific labor demands associated with late capitalism.

When policing agents favor good girls who follow normative structures, it forces at least some women to follow the norms closely so they could be recognized as good girls. Such good girls tend to be followers rather than rebels, thus helping factories develop a group of obedient, compliant workers who can be manipulated through benign patriarchal means. Controlling agents who make life intolerable and tiring also push workers out of factories just when they have become seasoned veterans who can stand up for workers' rights. That leads to factories hiring newer, less politically astute workers, which keeps wages low and ensures the factory regime does not get disrupted.

I therefore hold that despite rhetoric on modernization and empowerment, women find that they are still being judged based on nationalist gendered norms and expected to resist moral deregulation effectuated by trade deregulation. All this has led to their becoming marginalized players in macro and micro processes of global capitalism, nationalist resistance, and social class and identity struggles.

References

Alexander, R.M. (1998) *The Girl Problem: Female Sexual Delinquency in New York, 1900–1930*. Ithaca: Cornell University Press.

Dray-Novey, A. (1993) Spatial Order and Police in Imperial Beijing. *The Journal of Asian Studies*. 52 (4). pp. 885–922.

Enstad, N. (1999) *Ladies of Labor, Girls of Adventure: Working Women, Popular Culture and Labor Politics at the Turn of the Twentieth Century*. New York: Columbia University Press.

Fassin, D. (2013) *Enforcing Order: An Ethnography of Urban Policing*. Cambridge: Polity press.

Fu, D. (2009) A Cage of Voices: Producing and Doing Dagongmei in Contemporary China. *Modern China*. 35 (5). pp. 527–561.

Hewamanne, S. (2010) Suicide Narratives and In-Between Identities among Sri Lanka's Global Factory Workers. *Ethnology*. 49 (1). pp. 1–22.

Jackson, L.A. (2003) Care or Control?: The Metropolitan Women Police and Child Welfare, 1919–1969. *The Historical Journal*. 46 (3). pp. 623–648.

MacDowell Santos, Cecilia. (2005) *Women's Police Stations: Gender, Violence, and Justice in Sao Paulo*. London: Palgrave Macmillan.

Miller, J. and Carbone-Lopez, K. (2013) Gendered Carceral Regimes in Sri Lanka: Colonial Laws, Post-Colonial Practices, and the Social Control of Sex Workers. *Signs*. 39. pp. 79–103.

Odem, M.E. (1995) *Delinquent Daughters: Protecting and Policing Adolescent Female Sexuality in the United States, 1885–1920*. Chapel Hill: University of North Carolina Press.

Tambiah, Y. (2004) Sexuality and Women's Rights in Armed Conflict in Sri Lanka. *Reproductive Health Matters*. 12 (23). pp. 78–87.

Websdale, N. and Johnson, B. (2010) The Policing of Domestic Violence in Rural and Urban Areas: The Voices of Battered Women in Kentucky. *Policing and Society: An International Journal of Research and Policy*. 6 (4). pp. 297–317.

7 Man-power workers, contract workers, and Tamil workers

Sexual empowerment, from here to where?

"Desire is revolutionary in its essence."

(Deleuze and Guattari 1983: 116)

Many scholars have discussed how expressions of desire are a powerful politi-cal medium that reflect emotional and psychic empowerment as well as ongoing socio-cultural changes (Murray 1999; Ahearn 2003; Mankekar 2004; Gopinath 2005; Smith 2010). The previous chapters have focused on women workers' behavior, their narratives of desire, and actual relationships to highlight how the FTZ represents a potentially liberating space and how workers in different ways get involved in a process of becoming desiring subjects. Compared to what was permissible within the village environments they left, the anonymity of the FTZ affords a much freer space to seek connections and relations – be it romantic, sexual or social. While the women's accounts do not boast of a sexual liberation in an absolute sense – where they enjoyed sexual pleasure free of any constraining cultural, moral restrictions – they clearly indicate gradual changes in how women thought and acted after reaching the FTZ.

First, it is important to appreciate how these workers understood and expressed desire. Chapter 2 focused on how most women would not freely admit to sex-ual relations but performed their changed selves and desires within acceptable boundaries even while ensuring that they were able to save face if things went awry (which more often than not was the case). The chapter demonstrated why the un-utterability of sexual desire is hardly a reason to not discuss and analyze the new sexual subculture that has materialized within private and public spaces of the FTZ. One such subcultural performance was women's sexual banter with groups of men on Katunayake streets. Usually glossed over negatively as sexual harassment against women, this cross-group communication proved to be much more nuanced and layered. Women enjoyed participating in banter and consid-ered it an integral part of courtship preceding a relationship. While they enthu-siastically participated in NGO workshops designed to label and control public sexual banter, and use legal and moral vocabulary when it benefits them, most women described such banter as one of the most pleasurable aspects of FTZ living.

Chapter 3 demonstrated how sexual banter can be empowering for women in that these public performances represent a meaningful way for both working class men and women to articulate their right to city spaces notwithstanding the many regulatory forces surrounding them. It also argued that by uncritically adopting Western notions of sexual harassment to condemn sexual banter between working class men and women on city streets, NGOs and varied government agencies have unintentionally colluded in the capitalist global scheme to produce docile working class women who follow rules of respectability and thereby ensure an ideal assembly line workforce.

Chapter 4 focused on women reading and writing pornography within the FTZ and argued that this is in fact a critically feminist act that allow women workers identities outside the dominant mores of respectability. This chapter showed how FTZ workers read, discussed, and contributed to pornographic magazines and argued that their actions characterize a challenge to normative models of sexual behavior prescribed for rural women by dominant Sinhala Buddhist cultural discourses. Their contributions and the way they are depicted in others' stories in *Priyadari* evidence an alternative sexual culture that eludes social and psychic controls imposed on them by male and middle class agents and institutions. The chapter contends that pornographic magazines such as *Priyadari* can be a space where women's struggle for sexual agency finds voice, albeit within certain limitations. And just as NGO efforts that seek to curtail women's street banter promotes docile workers conducive to assembly line work, the prohibition and antagonism toward women reading and writing pornography also help produce "good, loyal, disciplined workers" who are ideal for global factories whose production targets are achieved via an obedient workforce of 'good girls' who follow rules and regulations.

Chapter 5 focused on a subject matter – militarization and war – that dominated Sri Lankan life for nearly three decades and analyzed its impact on FTZ workers' intimate lives. By delineating how nationalism, militarization, and class-based interests intersected to complicate women workers' struggle for sexual agency and conjugal happiness during and after the war, the chapter argued that both factory managers and the military treat women workers' labor (industrial and intimate) as cheap and easily disposable, leading to extra-legal, and therefore unredeemable, violence against women. While women do negotiate the best possible options within difficult circumstances, valorizing the soldiers' and workers' stigmatization present enormous obstacles to sexual agency and empowerment.

Chapter 6 discussed how the police, boarding house owners, and neighbors have appropriated guardian roles to control migrant women workers while trying to cement their class status. Much of the surveillance, condemnation, and punishments are based on conventional notions of female conduct and target the women for moral transgressions while absolving those who commit violence against them. The chapter evidenced how tensions occur when policing and disciplining get mired in nationalistic moral prescriptions and end up becoming a significant part of the social class and gendered difficulties that workers confront. In short, the agents and institutions supposed to protect and support the women workers become the very spaces and people women avoid. As one woman said, "When the fence and the demarcations (both supposed to protect the paddy) eat the paddy, to whom can we complain?" Again, their resistance to what powerful state and non-state agents want them to choose and comply with shows that the FTZ area allows for sexual expressions and fulfillment that their village environments do not. The fact that they had to engage with this sexual realm within an intense contestatory field render it acutely political and liberatory.

From here to where?: post war complications

Given the discussion in the preceding chapters, one would expect women's struggles to lose their intensity as society becomes more and more absorbed in a neoliberal worldview within which individual aspirations and improvements are supposed to trump over existing hierarchies and values. However, neoliberalism is working its dubious magic on contexts that are saturated with other cultural ideologies and structural conditions that are just as powerful. For instance, constant worker turnover at many global factories has led to labor recruiters now bringing workers from their own villages. Many of these workers are provided factory-run or supervised hostels and the recruiters promise shelter and protection for women, thereby making it easier for parents to send their daughters to the stigmatized FTZ. Nearly all Tamil women who have flocked to the FTZ after the war ended were brought by labor recruiters. The factories appear to treat them with more consideration, and the lifestyles and choices made available to them are pointedly different from the workers I have described earlier in this book. Additionally, so called man-power workers (part time workers), who get hired on a daily basis via man-power agents for auxiliary work, have also changed the dynamics within the FTZ. It is estimated that at present, about 30,000–35,000 workers in the apparel sector are recruited by manpower agencies.[1] Factories prefer such workers over hiring permanent workers who are prone to fight for their rights.[2] Both these new developments affect women's journeys toward sexual empowerment in complex ways.

As the labor recruiters are known to the parents, their promises hold more sway. The contractors' success in recruiting workers in turn depends on their track record. This has resulted in the "labor-recruiter brought workers" being cared for in unusually restrictive enclosures under the patriarchal gaze of matrons (and the contractors themselves who keep tabs on their behavior). The restrictions imposed seem to exceed the surveillance they lived under in their villages. While women enjoyed stress free lives in relatively comfortable living quarters and seemed to appreciate the same-sex sociability the factories and hostels afforded, they were being denied the social, commercial, and networking spaces and did not get the opportunities to develop decision-making skills by confronting difficult situations. Their lives, for the most part, seemed an extension of their village selves wherein they performed whatever tasks were asked of them while allowing important decisions to be taken by others.

The desires, pleasures, and intimate relationships that I described in earlier chapters were mostly dependent on women's ability to skillfully traverse different situations while making carefully balanced decisions about their sexual lives. The women who live protected lives under the watchful eyes of their labor contractor or matron do not find many opportunities to express their sexualities in public or private domains and could well return to their villages with just some monetary savings. Labor contractors are responsible for only a small portion of the FTZ worker population, but the number seems to be increasing every year. If at some point the majority of workers are those recruited and sheltered by labor contractors, the small revolutions in women workers' public and private intimate lives I have described earlier might get reversed. Because in such a context sexually transgressive workers will find it more difficult to seek anonymity within the sheltered and sexually non-expressive majority. Of course, there is always the possibility that with the passage of time these newly recruited women would rebel against labor contractors and boarding matrons to seek more independent lives.

It is also interesting to note how post civil war realities have affected the FTZ. Severe economic hardships experienced by all sections of society since the costly war ended have made FTZ employment less cost-effective than it used to be. Even as boarding house owners try to cover their increasing cost of living by unreasonable hikes in rents, the factories turn a blind eye to workers' cost of living expenses and keep their salaries low. The severe labor shortage experienced by low-paying factories has resulted in their use of labor contractors and the arrival of Tamil workers.

Working class Tamil women living in the northeast and on estates in the Central Province have in general dealt with severe economic hardships. The arid nature of the Northern Province especially was a principal reason for Northerners to migrate to other parts of the island seeking jobs. The civil war, which was mainly fought in the northeast, destroyed whatever industry was present and devastated livelihoods. Within this context, FTZ jobs can look very attractive to women whose only other employment option may be that of a day laborer. This has led to Tamil labor contractors transporting young Tamil women "by the busloads" (as one garment factory manager put it) to work in FTZ factories such as Star Garments and Christol Martin, which are owned or operated by Tamils. As per some Tamil workers, the Star Garments owner sent a recruiter in a car with an attached loud speaker to let those in his village know that a Tamil factory owner was hiring women. He made sure to promise that as a fellow villager he would take full responsibility to protect and shelter the young women when they got to Katunayake.

These Tamil women seem happier with their jobs than their Sinhala counterparts and also seem to appreciate their salaries and the opportunity to get away from economically stagnant, war-affected areas. Labor recruiters have negotiated special facilities at the boarding houses for these Tamil women, including higher boundary walls and more coverings for bathing facilities. Factory management also tread lightly around them to the extent of provoking envy among Sinhala workers. In one instance, the Star Garment owner provided a government-run model hostel a brand new flat screen TV so Tamil workers could watch Tamil channels, causing Sinhala women in the facility, who were stuck with an old

18 inch television, to be highly envious. One complained by saying that "Tamil workers seem to be the only ones who have human rights around here." Private boarding house owners the factory has contracted with have also been instructed to treat the Tamil workers kindly and sensitively and to learn to speak Tamil soon if they want to keep the lucrative contracts. The Tamil workers, the vast majority of whom only speak Tamil, appear to appreciate these gestures.

Many women recruited to Star Garments are housed at a government-run model hostel for females only. It is supervised by an older woman who is addressed as the matron. The Tamil and Sinhala women living there have to report whenever they leave and return to the hostel. No males are allowed within its walls, and that includes brothers and cousins. The matron and her assistant maintain a register that note when women begin and end their work shifts, which makes the monitoring process all the more rigorous. All residents have rotating responsibilities in maintaining the garden and tending flower beds. An outside caterer supplies their dinner, minimizing the time they have to spend shopping for groceries. Apparently, it is very difficult for these women to engage in public banter, read pornography, or meet men. In short, this is hardly an environment that allows sexual expressions to flourish.

If the Tamil workers and hostel conditions have altered the FTZ living environment for women workers, the increasing number of man-power workers have further complicated conditions. Factories are relying more and more on these daily wage, temporary (*aniyam*) workers in a bid to reduce the number of permanent workers who demand higher wages and rights. Some women find daily wage work profitable and convenient, as they get paid more in the short term and can choose when and when not to work. This flexibility comes at the expense of their developing political consciousness and precludes them from forming worker identities that their full time predecessors enjoy. Neither do they experience the boarding houses and the FTZ area as workers. Part time workers take long breaks from the FTZ area or work only a day or two a week, making life easier than for permanent workers. The latter have to return to difficult living conditions day after day, which pushes them out to the public spaces such as the railroad, the bazzar, and the market in search of social interactions across genders. Part time workers who take long breaks may not be that keen on finding community, social networking, and sexual gratification from the FTZ area. However, it is important to keep in mind that part time workers still constitute a minority within the FTZ. This makes it possible for sexual empowerment and a subculture to still thrive within the FTZ area.

Wither the subversive sexualities?

While upper middle class and rich Colombo youth attend night clubs and talk openly about dating and sex via social media, rural migrant women workers in Katunayake FTZ factories struggle to balance reputations with sexual desires. This happens as the FTZ itself goes through changes in labor demographics, recruiting, and living structures. Does this mean that women workers are heading toward living more sheltered lives within FTZ spaces? It is hard to predict. After all, the rural women who migrated to the FTZ for assembly line work and took up residence in houses with boarding aunties in charge were also not expected to become part of a sexual subculture. Yet, over the course of 30 years, the Katunay-ake FTZ area became synonymous with transgressive women. The new crop of labor contractor workers, part time workers, and Tamil workers may yet surprise us by developing their own trajectories toward becoming transgressive women.

There already seems to be some evidence of this. For instance, women are known to leave hostels because they find the conditions overly restricting. One woman ended up with an unwanted pregnancy after having had sex with the labor contractor. Tamil women forging romantic relationships with married Tamil men who work in jewelry shops in the area is being noted as an emerging problem. Such transgressions aside, one hears of women resisting and challenging in vari-ous settings. For instance, some Tamil women workers used the bark of a tree in the courtyard of the Catholic convent hostel they were housed at to paint an OM sign and conduct Hindu rituals. The Catholic nuns objected, but the women con-tinued decorating the tree with colorful flags and flower garlands while asking to be provided a more suitable place to perform religious rituals.

Workers who live together and share difficult conditions develop class con-sciousness in varied ways. The process may be different and slower for those living in hostels, especially when compared to the young Sinhala women who migrated on their own and lived with relatively less interference. Consequently, the way women living in hostels develop and express desires are bound to be dif-ferent, although their doing so will be no less interesting or risky. Studying such changes and challenges is important given the massive political, economic, and social changes the island is experiencing and the overarching cultural restrictions on sex and sexuality.

For instance, as recently as September 2015, a reproductive health awareness program demonstrated how difficult it was to even discuss reproduction – never mind sex. Chamila Thushari, the tireless project coordinator from Dabindu, expressed her frustration with workers who were not willing to openly engage in discussing reproduction by saying: "When asked about who in the audience engaged in sexual intercourse, not even the married women raised their hands because they feared they would have to talk about their experiences. No one shared any experiences. But they listened well and thanked us at the end for holding the workshop."[3] Interestingly, the women and men who participated in the workshop thereafter started calling the midwife at the Katunayake government health center who had conducted the lecture session. Callers anonymously admitted to having sexual relations and asked for advice on contraceptives, thus demonstrating the secrecy and silences surrounding issues pertaining to sex in a country that has one of the highest literacy rates in Asia.

These conditions make investigating the sexual politics of global workers more important than ever. As Judith Butler notes, when a child is assigned a gender, that child is encouraged to think, behave, and respond in certain ways. In that sense, the gender performativity does not presuppose an acting subject but a "complex convergence of social norms on a person's psyche. She writes, "If what 'I' want is only produced in relation to what is wanted from me, then the idea of 'my own' desire turns out to be something of a misnomer. I am, in my desire, negotiating what has been wanted of me." (2009: x–xi).

FTZ workers (and, for that matter any of us) may never be able to fully figure out what we desire. But FTZ workers stretch the boundaries of the intersection where what different actors want of them meet to produce desire. For instance, a FTZ worker who has a boyfriend may be privileging what her peer group wants above what she actually wants or what others may want/expect of her. In the same vein, when engaging in sex, workers can claim that they did so at the behest of their boyfriends. Some later recognize their own need for sexual pleasure and possession of another during foregone premarital sexual encounters. Within this context, how, when, and to what extent the individual figures in supposedly her own desire is hard to determine. As Varunika once noted: "Well, I fainted four times when he tried to have sex so that he knew I was a good girl. So that my girlfriends know that I resisted four times. All four times I was kind of interested too. When we finally had sex it was good. I liked it. Well, he left me after I got pregnant. I would not have ever told you that I enjoyed sex if not for the fact that it became kind of obvious that I had sex (becoming pregnant)," she said while laughing.

What is important is that this group of women constantly try to stretch the boundaries of what is permissible and, in the process, broaden the parameters governing female factory worker behavior. They have done so by challenging dominant cultural norms and patriarchy, and this is what makes their private sexual decisions and public activities acutely political and liberatory. Their activities are no small reason for the way gender and sexual norms within the island have been gradually changing over the past three decades. Many are quick to credit global cultural flows and Western-educated, middle class feminists for such ongoing changes, but doing so devalues the contributions made by the women I have discussed in this book. For it is they who have countered the forces (i.e., government officials, boarding house owners, and media) that have sought to constrain all women and, consequently, put their reputations and lives in danger. The fact is that cultural change cannot take place without rigid norms being challenged in a public arena under the media focus, and in Sri Lanka's case it is not elite women but those among the most marginalized that have taken the lead in doing so. This in no way suggests that drastic attitude changes or sane policies regarding reproductive rights or personal security have materialized, because that is still to be. But small changes have taken place. For instance several NGOs now conduct reproductive health camps and workshops and distribute free condoms in the FTZ area; a significant change in attitudes and practices from the early days of the FTZ.

Women continue to suffer violence in many forms due to wider society resisting their sexual choices and activities. But such opposition has not put a halt to their pursuing sexual agency. In fact, all evidence indicates that the FTZ sexual subculture – having boyfriends, engaging in premarital sex, denying having sex, and/or enjoying sexual pleasure – that I have described in this book has become more and more entrenched. The challenges and the workers' choices and strategies within precarious relationships have made them stronger, leading to improved negotiation skills, decision-making abilities, and creative thinking. Many such women have gone on to become entrepreneurs in their villages, a feat they would most likely not have attained if not for the FTZ experience. I assert that un-disciplined desires within the FTZ have helped them build non-conventional roles once back in their villages, roles that now gradually transform gender and social norms in Sri Lanka's countryside. This is what my next book, *Manipulating Capital: Sri Lanka's Former FTZ workers Negotiating Village Lives*, analyzes in detail.

Global workers' sexual lives are political, transformative, and empowering, and affect cultural and economic changes. This is what this book has sought to exemplify. It is indeed high time we recognize the political potential of supposedly private lives that groups like Sri Lanka's FTZ women workers are forced to enact in public arenas.

Notes

1 "Manpower Agencies Banned from FTZ." Leon Berenger. *The Sunday Times*. December 20, 2015. www.sundaytimes.lk/151220/news/manpower-agencies-banned-from-ftz-176004.html
2 The new chairman of the BOI, Mr. Upul Jayasuriya, stated at the Asian Floor Wage Alliance International Conference in Sri Lanka that the "man power agents will no longer be tolerated within the FTZ." www.sundaytimes.lk/151220/news/manpower-agencies-banned-from-ftz-176004.html. This does not include the private labor recruiters associated with individual factories, and in any case how this will be implemented remains to be seen.
3 Interview conducted on 09/30/2015

References

Ahearn, L. (2003) Writing Desire in Nepali Love Letters. *Language and Communication.* 23 (2). pp. 107–122.
Butler, J. (2009) AIBR. Revista de Antropología Iberoamericana. www.aibr.org Volumen 4, Número 3: i–xiii. Madrid: Antropólogos Iberoamericanos en.
Deleuze, G. and Guattari, F. (1983) *A Thousand Plateaus: Capitalism and Schizophrenia.* Minneapolis: University of Minnesota Press.
Gopinath, G. (2005) *Impossible Desires: Queer Diasporas and South Asian Public Cultures.* Durham: Duke University Press.
Mankekar, P. (2004) Dangerous Desires: Television and Erotics in Late Twentieth-Century India. *The Journal of Asian Studies.* 63 (2). pp. 403–431.
Murray, D. (1999) Laws of Desire?: Race, Sexuality and Power in Male Martinican Sexual Narratives. *American Ethnologist.* 26 (1). pp. 160–172.
Smith, M. (2010) Erasure of Sexuality and Desire: State Morality and Sri Lankan Migrants in Beirut, Lebanon. *The Asia Pacific Journal of Anthropology.* 11 (3–4). pp. 378–393.

Bibliography

Ahearn, L. (2003) Writing Desire in Nepali Love Letters. *Language and Communication.* 23 (2). pp. 107–122.

Alexander, R.M. (1998) *The Girl Problem: Female Sexual Delinquency in New York, 1900–1930.* Ithaca: Cornell University Press.

Arondekar, A. (2009) *For the Record: On Sexuality and the Colonial Archive in India.* Durham, NC: Duke University Press.

Barraclough, R. (2006) Tales of Seduction: Factory Girls in Korean Proletarian Literature. *Positions.* 14 (2). pp. 345–371.

Bender, D. (2004) Too Much of Distasteful Masculinity: Historicizing Sexual Harassment in the Garment Sweatshop and Factory. *Journal of Women's History.* 15 (4). pp. 91–116.

Berdahl, M. and Malone, D. (eds.) (2000) *Greed and Grievance: Economic Agendas in Civil Wars.* Boulder: Lynne Rienner.

Bose, B. (2008) Modernity, Globality, Sexuality, and the City: A Reading of Indian Cinema. *The Global South.* 2 (1). pp. 35–58.

Bourdieu, P. (1984) *Distinction: A Social Critique of the Judgement of Taste,* trans. by Richard Nice. London: Routledge.

Brow, J. (1999) Utopia's New-Found Space: Images of the Village Community in the Early Writings of Ananda Kumaraswamy. *Modern Asian Studies.* 33 (1). pp. 67–86.

Bularzik, M. (1983) Sexual Harassment at the Workplace: Historical Notes. In Green, J. (ed.). *Workers' Struggles, Past and Present: A Radical America Reader.* Philadelphia: Temple University Press. pp. 117–135.

Butler, J. (2009) AIBR. Revista de Antropología Iberoamericana. www.aibr.org Volumen 4, Número 3: i–xiii. Madrid: Antropólogos Iberoamericanos en.

Caldeira, T. (1999) Fortified Enclaves: The New Urban Segregation. In Low, S. (ed.). *Theorizing the City: The New Anthropology Reader.* New Brunswick: Rutgers University Press. pp. 83–110.

Chaitanya, K. (2006) Cost of War and Its Impact on the Sri Lankan Economy. In Fernando, L. (ed.). *Sri Lanka's Ethnic Conflict in the Global Context.* Colombo: Faculty of Graduate Studies. pp. 11–41.

Chatterjee, P. (1993) *The Nation and Its Fragments: Colonial and Post Colonial Histories.* Princeton: Princeton University Press.

Coulter, C. (2009) *Bush Wives and Girl Soldiers: Women's Lives through War and Peace in Sierra Leone.* Ithaca: Cornell University Press.

Dabindu Collective. (1997) *A Review of Free Trade Zones in Sri Lanka.* Boralesgamuwa: CRC Press.

De Alwis, M. (1997) The Production and Embodiment of Respectability: Gendered Demeanors in Colonial Ceylon. In Roberts, M. (ed.). *Sri Lanka Collective Identities Revisited.* Colombo: Marga Institute. pp. 105–144.

Deleuze, G. and Guattari, F. (1983) *A Thousand Plateaus: Capitalism and Schizophrenia*. Minneapolis: University of Minnesota Press.

De Mel, N. (2001) *Women and the Nation's Narrative: Gender and Nationalism in Twentieth Century Sri Lanka*. New Delhi: Kali for Women.

De Mel, N. (2003) Marketing War, Marketing Peace. Paper presented at the Workshop on "Home and the World: Changing Ethnic Identities in Sri Lanka" Colombo, Sri Lanka. June 18.

De Mel, N. (2003/04). Staging Pain: Representation, the Disabled Soldier and the Butterflies Theatre of Sri Lanka. *The Sri Lanka Journal of the Humanities*. 29–30 (1–2). pp. 111–129.

De Munck, Victor. (1996) Love and Marriage in a Sri Lankan Muslim Community: Toward a Reevaluation of Dravidian Marriage Practices. *American Ethnologist*. 23 (4). pp. 698–716.

De Munck, Victor. (1998) Lust, Love and Arranged Marriages in Sri Lanka. In De Munck, Victor (ed.). *Romantic Love and Sexual Behavior: Perspectives from the Social Sciences*. Connecticut: Praegar. pp. 285–300.

DeVotta, N. (ed.) (2005) *Benedictine Memoirs*. Talangama: JF&I Printers.

DeVotta, N. (2007) Strategizing Identities in a Civil War: Polyethnicity and Governance in Batticaloa. Paper presented at the Conference on Dialogue on Democracy and Pluralism in South Asia. New Delhi, India. May 1–2 2007.

Domosh, Mona. (1998) "Those Gorgeous Incongruities": Polite Politics and Public Space on the Streets of Nineteenth Century New York City. *Annals of the Association of American Geographers*. 88 (2). pp. 209–226.

Dray-Novey, A. (1993) Spatial Order and Police in Imperial Beijing. *The Journal of Asian Studies*. 52 (4). pp. 885–922.

Ehrlich, S. and King, R. (1996) Consensual Sex or Sexual Harassment: Negotiating Meaning. In Bergvall, V.L., Bing, J.M. and Freed, A.F. (eds.). *Rethinking Language and Gender Research: Theory and Practice*. London: Longman. pp. 153–172.

Enloe, C. (1983) *Does Khaki Become You?: The Militarization of Women's Lives*. Boston: South End Press.

Enloe, C. (2000) *Maneuvers: The International Politics of Militarizing Women's Lives*. Berkeley: University of California Press.

Enstad, N. (1999) *Ladies of Labor, Girls of Adventure: Working Women, Popular Culture and Labor Politics at the Turn of the Twentieth Century*. New York: Columbia University Press.

Fassin, D. (2013) *Enforcing Order: An Ethnography of Urban Policing*. Polity press.

Fernandez-Kelly, M.P. (1983) *For We are Sold, I and My People*. Albany: SUNY Press.

Foucault, M. (1978) *The History of Sexuality*, Volume 1. New York: Vintage.

Freeman, C. (2000) *High Tech and High Heels in the Global Economy: Women, Work, and Pink-Collar Identities in the Caribbean*. Durham: Duke University Press.

Fu, D. (2009) A Cage of Voices: Producing and Doing Dagongmei in Contemporary China. *Modern China*. 35 (5). pp. 527–561.

Giles, W. and Hyndman, J. (eds.) (2004) *Sites of Violence: Gender and Conflict Zones*. Berkeley: University of California Press.

Giuffre, P.A. (1997) Labeling Sexual Harassment in Hospitals: A Case Study of Doctors and Nurses. Paper Presented at the Sociologists Against Sexual Harassment Meeting. Toronto, Canada.

Giuffre, P.A. and Williams, C.L. (1994) Boundary Lines: Labeling Sexual Harassment in Restaurants. *Gender and Society*. 8. pp. 378–401.

Gopinath, G. (2005) *Impossible Desires: Queer Diasporas and South Asian Public Cultures*. Durham: Duke University Press.

Greenberg, D. (1995) The Pleasures of Homosexuality. In Abramson, P. and Pinkerton, S. (eds.). *Sexual Nature, Sexual Culture*. Chicago: University of Chicago Press. pp. 223–256.

Gruber, J. (1998) The Impact of Male Work Environments and Organizational Policies on Women's Experiences of Sexual Harassment. *Gender & Society*. 12. pp. 301–320.

Gunawardana, S. (2010) What Does Transnational Solidarity Mean for Sri Lanka's Migrant Women Workers? In Bieler, A. and Lindberg, I. (eds.). *Transnational Solidarity in Times of Global Restructuring: Prospects for New Alliances across Borders*. London: Routledge. pp. 87–100.

Guruge, A. (1965) *Anagarika Dharmapala: Return to Righteousness*. Colombo: Government Press.

Hettiarachchy, T. and Schensul, S.L. (2001) The Risks of Pregnancy and the Consequences among Young Unmarried Women Working in a Free Trade Zone in Sri Lanka. *Asia Pacific Population Journal*. 16 (2). pp. 25–140.

Hewamanne, S. (2003) Performing Disrespectability: New Tastes, Cultural Practices and Identity Performances by Sri Lanka's Free Trade Zone Garment Factory Workers. *Cultural Dynamics*. 15 (1). pp. 71–101.

Hewamanne, S. (2006) Pornographic Voice: Critical Feminist Practices among Sri Lanka's Garment Factory Workers. *Feminist Studies*. 32 (1). pp. 125–154.

Hewamanne, S. (2008a) *Stitching Identities in a Free Trade Zone: Gender and Politics in Sri Lanka*. Philadelphia: University of Pennsylvania Press.

Hewamanne, S. (2008b) "City of Whores": Nationalism, Development and Global Garment Workers of Sri Lanka. *Social Text*. 95 (2). pp. 35–59.

Hewamanne, S. (2009) Duty Bound?: Militarization, Romances and New Spaces of Violence among Sri Lanka's Free Trade Zone Garment Factory Workers. *Cultural Dynamics*. 21 (2). pp. 153–184.

Hewamanne, S. (2010a) Suicide Narratives and In-Between Identities among Sri Lanka's Global Factory Workers. *Ethnology*. 49 (1). pp. 1–22.

Hewamanne, S. (2010b) Gendering the Internally Displaced: Problem Bodies, Fluid Boundaries and Politics of Civil Society Participation in Sri Lanka. *International Journal of Women's Studies*. 11 (1). pp. 157–172.

Hewamanne, S. (2012) Negotiating Sexual Meanings: Global Discourses, Local Practices and Free Trade Zone Workers on City Streets. *Ethnography*. 13 (3). pp. 352–374.

Hewamanne, S. (2013) The War Zone in My Heart: The Occupation of Southern Sri Lanka. In Visweswaran, K. (ed.). *Everyday Occupations: Gender and Militarization in South Asia*. Philadelphia: University of Pennsylvania Press. pp. 60–84.

Hewamanne, S. (2015) Complicated Belonging: Gendered Empowerment and Anxieties about 'Returning' among Internally Displaced Muslim Women in Puttalam, Sri Lanka. In Ahmed Ghosh, H. (ed.). *Walking the Tight Rope: Gender and Islam in Asia*. Albany: State University of New York Press. pp. 61–82.

Hyndman, J. (2000) *Managing Displacement: Refugees and the Politics of Humanitarianism*. Minneapolis: University of Minnesota Press.

Jackson, L.A. (2003) Care or Control?: The Metropolitan Women Police and Child Welfare, 1919–1969. *The Historical Journal*. 46 (3). pp. 623–648.

Jeganathan, P. (2002) Walking Through Violence: Everyday life and Anthropology. In Mines, D. and Lamb, S. (eds.). *Everyday Life in South Asia*. Bloomington: Indiana University Press. pp. 357–365.

Jensen, B. (2005) Bawdy Bodies or Moral Agency?: The Struggle for Identity in Working Class Autobiographies of Imperial Germany. *Biography*. 28 (4). pp. 534–557.

Jordal, Malin, Wijewardena, Kumudu, Ohman, Ann, Essen, Brigitta, and Olsson, Pia. (2014) Negotiating Respectability: Migrant Women Workers' Perceptions of Relationships and

Sexuality in Free Trade Zones in Sri Lanka. *Health Care for Women International.* 35. pp. 658–676.

Kondo, D. (1997) *About Face: Performing Race in Fashion and Theater.* New York: Routledge.

Lerum, K. (2004) Sexuality, Power and Camaraderie in Service Work. *Gender and Society.* 18 (6). pp. 756–776.

Loe, M. (1996) Working for Men – At the Intersection of Power, Gender and Sexuality. *Social Inquiry.* 66. pp. 399–421.

Lorde, A. (2007) Uses of the Erotic: The Erotic as Power. In *Sister Outsider: Essays and Speeches by Audrey Lorde.* Berkeley: Crossing Press. pp. 53–59.

Low, S. (2000) *On the Plaza: The Politics of Public Space and Culture.* Austin: University of Texas Press.

Low, S. (2001) The Edge and the Center: Gated Communities and the Discourse of Urban Fear. *American Anthropologist.* 103 (1). pp. 45–58.

Luff, D. (2001) The Down Right Torture of Women: Moral Lobby Women, Feminists and Pornography. *The Sociological Review.* 49 (1). pp. 78–99.

Lutz, C. (2002) The Wars Less Known. *The South Atlantic Quarterly.* 101 (2). pp. 285–296.

Lynch, C. (2004) Economic Liberalization, Nationalism and Women's Morality in Sri Lanka. In Winslow, D. and Woost, M. (eds.). *Economy, Culture and Civil War in Sri Lanka.* Bloomington: Indiana University Press. pp. 168–191.

MacDowell Santos, Cecilia. (2005) *Women's Police Stations: Gender, Violence, and Justice in Sao Paulo.* London: Palgrave Macmillan.

MacKinnon, C.A. (1979) *Sexual Harassment of Working Women: A Case of Sexual Discrimination.* New Haven: Yale University Press.

Manderson, L. and Aggleton, P. (2003) Belief Systems and the Place of Desire: Perspectives from Asia and the Pacific. Editorial Introduction. *Culture, Health & Sexuality.* 5 (3). pp. 181–184.

Mankekar, P. (2004) Dangerous Desires: Television and Erotics in Late Twentieth-Century India. *The Journal of Asian Studies.* 63 (2). pp. 403–431.

Miller, J. and Carbone-Lopez, K. (2013) Gendered Carceral Regimes in Sri Lanka: Colonial Laws, Post-Colonial Practices, and the Social Control of Sex Workers. *Signs.* 39. pp. 79–103.

Mills, M.B. (1999) *Thai Women in the Global Labor Force: Consuming Desires: Contested Selves.* New Brunswick: Rutgers University Press.

Modleski, T. (1982) *Loving With a Vengeance: Mass Produced Fantasies for Women.* Connecticut: Archon Books.

Moore, M. (1985) *The State and Peasant Politics in Sri Lanka.* Cambridge: Cambridge University Press.

Morris, R.C. (1995) All Made Up: Performance Theory and the New Anthropology of Sex and Gender. *Annual Review of Anthropology.* 24. pp. 567–592.

Murray, D. (1999) Laws of Desire?: Race, Sexuality and Power in Male Martinican Sexual Narratives. *American Ethnologist.* 26 (1). pp. 160–172.

Narayan, K. (1993) Banana Republics and V.I. Degrees: Rethinking Indian Folklore in a Postcolonial World. *Asian Folklore Studies.* 52. pp. 177–204.

Nead, L. (1993) Above the Pulpline: The Cultural Significance of Erotic Art. In Gibson, P. and Gibson, R. (eds.). *Dirty Looks: Women, Pornography, Power.* London: BFI. pp. 144–155.

Obeyesekere, G. (1975) Sorcery, Premeditated Murder and the Canalization of Aggression in Sri Lanka. *Ethnology.* 14 (1). pp. 1–23.

Obeyesekere, G. (1984) *The Cult of the Goddess Pattini*. Chicago: University of Chicago Press.

Odem, M.E. (1995) *Delinquent Daughters: Protecting and Policing Adolescent Female Sexuality in the United States, 1885–1920*. Chapel Hill: University of North Carolina Press.

Osella, C. and Osella, F. (1998) Friendship and Flirting: Micro-Politics in Kerala, South India. *Journal of the Royal Anthropological Institute*. 4. pp. 189–206.

Peiss, K. (1986) *Cheap Amusements: Working Women and Leisure in Turn of the Century New York*. Philadelphia: Temple University Press.

Pena, D. (1997) *The Terror of the Machine: Technology, Work, Gender and Ecology on the U.S.-Mexico Border*. Austin: University of Texas.

Plotnicov, L. (1995) Love, Lost and Found in Nigeria. In Jankowiak, W. (ed.). *Romantic Passion: A Universal Experience*. New York: Columbia University Press. pp. 128–140.

Pun, N. (2005) *Made in China: Women Factory Workers in a Global Workplace*. Durham: Duke University Press.

Radway, J. (1984) *Reading the Romance: Women, Patriarchy and Popular Literature*. Chapel Hill: The University of North Carolina Press.

Ruwanpura, E. (2011a) Sex or Sensibility? The Making of Chaste Women and Promiscuous Men in a Sri Lankan University Setting (*The University of Edinburgh*, 2011–11–22).

Ruwanpura, K. (2011b) *Ethical Codes: Reality and Rhetoric: A Study of Sri Lanka's Apparel Sector*. University of Southampton: Report for the Economic and Social Research Council.

Salzinger, L. (2000) Manufacturing Sexual Subjects: "Harassment", Desire and Discipline on a Maquiladora Shop floor. *Ethnography*. 1. pp. 67–92.

Salzinger, L. (2003) *Genders in Production: Making Workers in Mexico's Global Factories*. Berkley: University of California Press.

Segal, L. (1993) Does Pornography Cause Violence?: The Search for Evidence. In Gibson, P. and Gibson, R. (eds.). *Dirty Looks: Women, Pornography, Power*. London: British Film Institute. pp. 5–21.

Shah, S. (2014) *Street Corner Secrets: Sex, Work, and Migration in the City of Mumbai*. Durham: Duke University Press.

Silva, K. Tudor and Eisenberg, Merrill. (1996) Attitude Toward Pre-marital Sex in a Sample of Sri Lankan Youth. Paper presented at the National Convention on Women's Studies, Center for Women's Research. Sri Lanka.

Smart, A. (2001) Unruly Places: Urban Governance and the Persistence of Illegality in Hong Kong's Urban Squatter Areas. *American Anthropologist*. 103 (1). pp. 30–44.

Smith, M. (2010) Erasure of Sexuality and Desire: State Morality and Sri Lankan Migrants in Beirut, Lebanon. *The Asia Pacific Journal of Anthropology*. 11 (3–4). pp. 378–393.

Srivastava, S. (ed.) (2004) *Sexual Sites, Seminal Attitudes: Sexualities, Masculinities and Culture in South Asia*. London: Sage.

Staudt, K. and Mendez, Z. (2015) *Courage, Resistance and Women in Ciudad Juarez: Challenges to Militarization*. Austin: The University of Texas Press.

Strategic Foresight Group. (2006) *Cost of Conflict in Sri Lanka*. Mumbai: Strategic Foresight Group.

Thiranagama, S. (2013) *In My Mother's House: Civil War in Sri Lanka*. Philadelphia: University of Pennsylvania Press.

Uggen, C. and Blackstone, A. (2004) Sexual Harassment as a Gendered Expression of Power. *American Sociological Review*. 69. pp. 64–92.

Utas, M. (2005) Victimcy, Girlfriending, Soldiering: Tactic Agency in a Young Woman's Social Navigation of the Liberian War Zone. *Anthropological Quarterly* 78 (2). pp. 403–430.

Vanita, R. (ed.) (2002) *Queering India: Same Sex Love and Eroticism in Indian Culture and Society*. New York: Routledge.

Vigil, A. (2014) *War Echoes: Gender and Militarization in U.S. Latina/o Cultural Production*. New Jersey: Rutgers University Press.

Visweswaran, K. (ed.) (2013) *Everyday Occupations: Experiencing Militarism in South Asia and the Middle East*. Philadelphia: University of Pennsylvania Press.

Websdale, N. and Johnson, B. (2010) The Policing of Domestic Violence in Rural and Urban Areas: The Voices of Battered Women in Kentucky. *Policing and Society: An International Journal of Research and Policy*. 6 (4). pp. 297–317.

Wijayatilake, K. (2004) *Study on Sexual and Gender Based Violence in Selected Locations in Sri Lanka*. Colombo: CENWOR.

Williams, C., Giuffre, P., and Dellinger, K. (1999) Sexuality in the Workplace: Organizational Control, Sexual Harassment, and the Pursuit of Pleasure. *Annual Review of Sociology*. 25. pp. 73–93.

Willis, P. (1993) Symbolic Creativity. In Gray, A. and McGuigan, J. (eds.). *Studying Culture: An Introductory Reader*. London: Edward Arnold. pp. 108–120.

Winslow, D. and Woost, M. (2004) Introduction. In Winslow, D. and Woost, M. (eds.). *Economy, Culture and Civil War in Sri Lanka*. Bloomington: Indiana University Press.

Wolf, D. (1992) *Factory Daughters: Gender, Household Dynamics and Rural Industrialization in Java*. Berkeley: University of California Press. pp. 1–31.

Yelvington, K. (1996) Flirting in the Factory. *Journal of Royal Anthropological Institution*. 31. pp. 119–165.

Yuval-Davis, N. (1997) *Gender and Nation*. London: Sage.

Yuval-Davis, N. (2012) *The Politics of Belonging: Intersectional Contestations*. London: Sage.

Zacharias, U. (2001) Trial by Fire: Gender, Power and Citizenship in Narratives of the Nation. *Social Text*. 19 (4). pp. 29–51.

Index